Strategic Defense and the
American Ethos

The Johns Hopkins Foreign Policy Institute (FPI) was founded in 1980 and serves as the research center for the School of Advanced International Studies (SAIS) in Washington, D.C. The FPI is a meeting place for SAIS faculty members and students as well as for government analysts, policymakers, diplomats, journalists, business leaders, and other specialists in international affairs. In addition to conducting research on policy-related international issues, the FPI sponsors conferences, seminars, and roundtables.

The FPI's research activities are often carried out in conjunction with SAIS's regional and functional programs dealing with Latin America and the Caribbean Basin, U.S. foreign policy, U.S.-Japan relations, Canada, Africa, Europe, security studies, international energy, and international economics.

FPI publications include the *SAIS Review*, a biannual journal of foreign affairs, which is edited by SAIS students; the SAIS Papers in International Affairs, a monograph series copublished with Westview Press in Boulder, Colorado; and the FPI Policy Briefs, a series of analyses of immediate or emerging foreign-policy issues.

Strategic Defense and the American Ethos: Can the Nuclear World Be Changed? is the second in a series of five books. This series is being prepared by the FPI as part of a research project on the long-term implications of military programs and activities in space for strategic stability, superpower relations, and alliance cohesion.

For additional information regarding FPI publications, write to: FPI Publications Program, School of Advanced International Studies, The Johns Hopkins University, 1740 Massachusetts Avenue, NW, Washington, DC 20036.

ABOUT THE BOOK AND AUTHOR

The concept and utility of strategic defense should be evaluated in an embracing cultural context defined by the values, attitudes, and worldview of society—its ethos. The Strategic Defense Initiative (SDI) responds both to changes in the American ethos and to shifts in the balance of power. Together, these changes have undermined the basis of U.S. force posture and alliance relationships in the nuclear era: deterrence through the threat of nuclear retaliation. Dr. Vlahos argues that SDI offers an escape from a strategic cul-de-sac and provides an alternative to a national security policy many Americans believe to be unworkable. Those Americans who reject SDI do so on the grounds that it is technologically infeasible or that only arms control—not more weapons—can secure peace. Yet even less-than-perfect defenses could serve important limited goals, according to Dr. Vlahos. Initially, limited defenses could enhance deterrence, and as defenses evolved, they might reshape the strategic environment, shifting the emphasis of U.S.-Soviet competition away from ballistic missiles and the primacy of offensive nuclear forces.

This book links the larger cultural process from which strategic posture is ultimately derived to the utility of strategic defenses. If strategic defenses are a product of cultural pressures, they must also promote the goal of such pressures: enhanced national security. This is the promise of SDI.

Michael Vlahos is codirector of the Security Studies Program at The Johns Hopkins School of Advanced International Studies (SAIS). He is also a research professor of security studies at SAIS and staff consultant to The Johns Hopkins Applied Physics Laboratory. His previous books include *The Blue Sword: The Naval War College and the American Mission, 1919–1941* (1981) and *America: Images of Empire* (1982).

SAIS PAPERS IN INTERNATIONAL AFFAIRS

Strategic Defense and the American Ethos

Can the Nuclear World Be Changed?

Michael Vlahos

WESTVIEW PRESS/BOULDER AND LONDON
WITH THE FOREIGN POLICY INSTITUTE
SCHOOL OF ADVANCED INTERNATIONAL STUDIES
THE JOHNS HOPKINS UNIVERSITY

A Westview Press / Foreign Policy Institute Edition

This Westview softcover edition is printed on acid-free paper and bound in softcovers that carry the highest rating of the National Association of State Textbook Administrators, in consultation with the Association of American Publishers and the Book Manufacturers' Institute.

Copyright © 1986 by The Johns Hopkins Foreign Policy Institute, School of Advanced International Studies (SAIS)

Published in 1986 in the United States of America by Westview Press, Inc.; Frederick A. Praeger, Publisher; 5500 Central Avenue, Boulder, Colorado 80301

Library of Congress Catalog Card Number: 86-28990
ISBN: 0-8133-0466-0

Composition for this book was provided by The Magazine Group, Inc., Washington, D.C., for The Johns Hopkins Foreign Policy Institute, SAIS.
This book was produced without formal editing by the publisher.

Printed and bound in the United States of America

The paper used in this publication meets the requirements of the American National Standard for Permanence of Paper for Printed Library Materials Z39.48-1984.

6   5   4   3   2   1

CONTENTS

ACKNOWLEDGMENTS

There are many people I wish to thank: Harold Brown, for giving me incentive; Paul Nitze and Simon Serfaty, for their support; Bruce Valley, Adam Garfinkle, Dan Gouré, Charles Fairbanks, Bob Osgood, Tom Evans, and Bruce Jackson, who selflessly read through draft after draft; Nancy McCoy, for her limpidity of thought; and, last, my father, who helped me find my voice.

INTRODUCTION

America is talking again about how to defend itself from attack. For decades, since Hiroshima, this nation has wrestled with the possible consequences of a war in which nuclear weapons were launched against the United States. With the advent of the hydrogen bomb, we faced the prospect of potential national extinction if such weapons hit America. Still, we tried to defend against these terrible things. Had we any choice? Could we rely on the restraint of our sworn enemy and yield our security—even our survival—to a trust that nuclear weapons would not be used?

Of course not. We tried to develop defenses, aircraft and missiles that would shoot down the bombers that could attack the United States with nuclear bombs. Then came the ICBM— *Sputnik*—the intercontinental ballistic missile. Against this weapon, arcing into space and back at hypersonic speed, there was no defense.

There was an alternative doctrine, a simple concept really, that could substitute for real defenses. This was a doctrine called deterrence. It meant, quite simply, that the United States would deter nuclear attack with the threat of disproportionate counterattack. If the Soviet Union launched nuclear missiles at the United States, we would retaliate by launching nuclear missiles back at them. We would threaten their ultimate destruction. Although we might not initially respond by destroying the Soviet Union, we would do so if the Soviets attempted to incinerate America.

The Soviets would gain nothing from their awesome power to destroy the United States. We could not gain by threatening to destroy them. Neither party would benefit from nuclear use. Nuclear war could not be "won" if both sides were destroyed. Checkmate. Deterrence works.

The problem, however, was not so simple as the concept. It was complicated by how America redefined the geography of national security after global war. After 1945 it was no longer possible for Americans to equate national security with merely a North American continent or even Western Hemisphere free from attack. The United States got into the business of defending something called a Free World. We had become our brother's keeper, at least for the community of democratic peoples.

We defended this world with nuclear weapons. Throughout the 1950s we declared that the United States could use atomic bombs if freedom was abridged anywhere in the world. Since that time we have softened publicly the conditions under which America might use nuclear weapons to defend its allies. In addition, by the 1970s the number of our allies had dwindled, and our commitment to defend to the death had shrunk to NATO Europe, Japan and the Republic of Korea, and Australasia.

But defending others with nuclear weapons implied the distinct possibility that using them would lead to the ultimate nuclear use: what came to be known as mutual assured destruction (MAD), the very heart of deterrence itself. This possibility made any crisis between the United States and the Soviet Union in the public mind the potential "first step" to "nuclear holocaust."

Add to this apprehension the growth in Soviet nuclear strength. There had been a time, enshrouded in myth for many today, when only the United States possessed "the bomb." Then there was a generation or so when the Soviets had bombs, but of a kind and number and delivery distinctly inferior to the U.S. nuclear arsenal. This meant that the same generation of Americans could have confidence in the very scary concept of deterrence because it was a concept that we controlled. We were stronger. We had the choice of weapons, and the field.

The theory of deterrence has been rooted in two assumptions: U.S. nuclear superiority and the extension of deterrence—the will to escalate from conventional war—that only U.S. nuclear superiority can guarantee with confidence. Now there is no such confidence. The Soviet nuclear buildup has exposed the fragility of deterrence without strategic advantage. The United States has been unable to keep pace with recent Soviet nuclear programs. It has been unable to restrain them through arms control. It has been unable to counter them with sufficient new nuclear programs.

The issue of strategic defense is really an issue of change. More important, it is also change in the readiness of the American people to endure a strategy that can no longer promise security.

Debate over "Star Wars" is a struggle over unspoken values. It is a part of a tension stretching back to America's beginnings. One part is a tension over the proper American role in the wider world. Can we forever defend other peoples on the basis of inevitable American destruction? Another part is a tension over the very nature of our national security. Can we continue to trust our way of life to a strategic concept of retaliation that is believed both immoral and unworkable?

The president's Strategic Defense Initiative (SDI) was presented as a visionary fork in the road. It may never bring us back to a former time when we felt safe from attack, when our security seemed to rest on our free will. It is nonetheless a potential turning point for Americans.

SDI is not just another future weapons system. It is both an instrument and a signal of historical change. Strategic defense did not reemerge as a result of technology alone. Its appeal is not in the eyes of bureaucrats searching for efficiencies, or of a Congress bedazzled by pork barrels, or of generals staking claim to more turf. Defense against nuclear attack has emerged from an eroding American strategic position, a stance that many believe is losing the respect of allies and adversary and, at last, of Americans themselves.

The surface debate may look like just another arcane tug-of-war in the Washington strategic community. It is not. The Strategic Defense Initiative is a response to something much bigger.

This essay seeks to tie deeper currents in American national security to current problems in U.S. nuclear strategy and then, finally, to imagine a world with defenses—a world more consonant with the American national ethos. Discussions of national security tend to be parochial. They are insulated from the culture that provides their mandate. The influences of society are often ignored by strategists.

A conventional approach to strategic defenses and American national security would focus on the strict utility of potential systems. It would do so within goals given by national strategy as it evolved after 1945. Would defenses strengthen deterrence? What would be alternative U.S. deterrent postures at varying levels of defensive capability?

But this piece will not hew to convention. If the issue of strategic defense has indeed emerged from change in the nuclear world, a shaking of tradition, then its origins must be probed. The first part of this exploration looks at the American past. This is a place that few in the strategic community visit. But our ultimate architecture of national security will be shaped by the needs of American culture, however unpalatable this may seem to strategic thinkers.

Many questions must be asked. How did persistent national attitudes lead to the Strategic Defense Initiative? Are there traditions in the American style of national security that have found voice in strategic defenses? Is SDI an authentic expression of the American ethos?

Technology has recently encouraged a rethinking of defense against nuclear missiles. If new defensive technology had been incorporated into traditional deterrence doctrine, defenses could have been pursued to strengthen deterrence and in part avoid the loss of confidence in the doctrine itself. Why not? Why was it left to a visonary presidential speech to set a course ahead? How and why did a national consensus committed to nuclear deterrence splinter? Why did change in the nuclear world lead to the Reagan vision and not to an attempt to shore up tradition?

It is my thesis that an impending American cultural rejection of a strategy of deterrence through the promise of mutual annihilation led to renewed interest in strategic defenses. Defenses in turn became construed as a deus ex machina, an easy way out of the nuclear dilemma. After examining these trends, I attempt to explore how a world with defenses against ICBMs would work, to see whether defenses could fulfill the changing mandate of American culture.

There are problems with even attempting such versification. In response to change, alternative futures are straightforward but culturally elusive. The power of present reality is tenacious. It is difficult even to think about a future that might diverge from today's norms. The dominance of the status quo is like a rock. It is easy to imagine the maintenance of deterrence along traditional lines, in which very limited defenses might help to preserve deterrence. It is difficult to explore a future in which defenses change the strategic context. Many wish actually to prevent such exploration. Yet if it is possible that broad changes in American culture are beginning to demand detachment from the iron maiden of MAD, then the choices in alternative futures must be confronted. The second part of this book is a glimpse into a future in which defenses, however imperfect, rob the offense of its current sway over the strategic balance.

Many in Washington believe that a world dominated by defenses is the least likely of possible futures. For them, the tradition of offensive nuclear forces is too strong to alter. But it must be imagined. How should a world with strong strategic defenses be described? How would such a world work in terms of strategic competition? Would it be truly a "defended world," as suggested by President Reagan? If not, would it be enough simply to change the language of strategic competition away from MAD? What elements would be needed to make such a world appealing to the American ethos?

The very strategic community that seeded and nurtured nuclear deterrence is now called upon to judge a major revision of its doctrine. We should understand that for the members of this community the most attractive approaches might also be the most modulated, the most finely tuned. It is difficult to discuss change if change is unwanted. It is even harder to face if change implies a rejection of one's own work.

Deterrence through threat of nuclear retaliation has kept the peace for forty years. It has not failed. The deaths of hundreds of millions have not been entered on its ledger. But it is in the process of cultural rejection by Americans. Change cannot be forever delayed. It is my hope to examine its origins and its future.

PAST

1.
AMERICAN ETHOS AND NATIONAL SECURITY

National-security policies reflect the culture of the society creating them. The culture of a society—its ethos—defines distinctive patterns of individual and group behavior. Culture shapes the way we look at the world: our worldview. Whatever our immediate group membership, our final sense of identity is shaped by larger cultural patterns. Each human culture is unique, and each society's forms of war and politics express this uniqueness.[1]

The United States has taken this truth as its own. From the beginning this nation imposed upon itself a self-conscious identity in contrast to the European world. It was a "New World" torn from the "Old." Americans need to strengthen their self-described uniqueness, and our national-security policy has always been asked to reinforce our identity.

National security in American life exists as an icon and instrumentality lying between the Old World and the New. Society has shaped its armed forces not simply to defend, but to represent America and serve as the physical mechanism of its separation from or involvement in the larger world.[2]

The issue of separation or involvement is central to the American experience. It has created continuing tension over the use of military force. It is a force pulling against itself, a tension at the root of the American mission. America is marked by its sense of mission, for it was a concept before it was a place, and a place before it was a nation. America began as a sanctuary, a religious and political refuge from European tyranny, Americans have defined themselves according to the charge of a national "mission." America was both removed from Europe and created by Europeans. It existed as a refuge from all that was evil there, but also as a symbol of Europe's eventual reformation. The United States has a national mission that is both protective and proselytizing. But which interpretation of national mission will prevail?

This fundamental stress can be called a struggle between "progress" and "purification." It is a conflict over the direction of national identity. What we are is dependent on what we will be. America is a concept forever in the process of "becoming." Where we are going is the key to becoming. The right path must be taken. And there have always been two righteous paths for America. Calling them "progressive" and "purifier" is not meant to imply formal, or even conscious political affiliation in the galaxy of American interest groups. But it is a way of describing how all Americans, at the unspoken core of their meaning, speak in ways that form significant variations within the common sense of what it is to be an American.

This dualistic identity shares common religious roots. The impact of Protestant thought is felt in the ways we talk about mission, service, sacrifice, restraint. It underlies the sense that Americans share as serving a higher calling. If America's core values can be defined, they would begin with this sense of calling. It is linked to the broader and secular notion of national mission.

Both progressive and purifier visions of national identity also began with the belief that America was to be the temporal enactment of God's will and purpose. The progressive focused on national becoming through physical experience: manifest destiny. The purifier saw an American realization through spiritual example, as in American Christian missionary movements.[3]

The progressive part of our ethos calls for a literal realization of national mission. From the beginning, mission involved a place. This place was called many things, from an American "empire" to a "New Jerusalem." At first it was an alternative world to the tyranny of Europe. Eventually the progressive New World sought to reform the Old.

The key is that American values and goals are to be realized through the physical growth of the United States. Nineteenth-century expansion was territorial. Twentieth-century expansion was contractual. The United States became committed to the world.

For the progressive, there is a role for war: War can be both just and necessary. In the American Revolution, war created liberty. In the Civil War, war preserved it. American intervention in the two world wars rescued humanity. War is fought both to defend America and to realize its mission. The horrifying weapons of the nuclear age were wedged reluctantly within this tradition.

War is seen as corrupting. Progressives, however, believe that the American calling is righteous enough to defy war's corruption. This will be true as long as the American way of war is true to the American ethos.[4]

Theodore Roosevelt embodied the progressive approach to war and military force. For Roosevelt, this approach actually mirrored a self-styled, "progressive" domestic political agenda. Roosevelt put strategy into practice. U.S. military power was used to promote world stability, and U.S. naval forces became an active instrument of an American mission. This set a twentieth-century precedent.[5]

The other cause is no less "righteous." It can demand more of American society. The purifier demands that the United States attain earthly perfection before it preaches to others. Reform thyself, and be a model to the world. The power of American virtue will spread the word. The United States will uplift through example.

For the purifiers, American expansion means war. War is always morally corrosive. There is no defense against its poison. The growth of the United States in the 1840s was seen as an extension of slavery. Expansion in the 1890s perpetuated an unjust economic system. Today, America's "global reach" is called an economic enslavement of the Third World.

Daniel Webster said it all: "You have a Sparta, embellish it!" He meant that America lives in the uprightness of its citizens, that spiritual purity is in inverse proportion to physical size, that an American empire would equal imperialism, and that physical expansion would destroy American democracy and the American soul.[6]

The impulse to national expansion is seen as an expression of domestic disease. It is a symptom that our society is in need of healing.

Purifiers are not always pacifists. Their suspicion of military establishments is an American tradition. In eighteenth-century Europe, armies were the agents of monarchy and the tools of tyranny. The original American army was the militia. It was the first "peoples" army. In contrast, a large standing military was seen as a separate political force in society. It would "militarize" America and promote war. In this sense purifiers hearken to the America of the 1790s.[7]

There is no formal allegiance by groups as progressives or purifiers. Interest groups in society tend to have special concerns. They consider an embracing American mission only when parts of it connect with their own objectives. The very words "purifier" and "progressive" describe two basic approaches to an American sense of mission. The core values are shared—constitution, democracy, economic opportunity, a conviction of the universal rightness of the values themselves—but the path to promoting or safeguarding them differs profoundly. Groups in U.S. society tend to lean toward either the purifier or the progressive, without using those terms. Most individuals and groups think in terms of political allegiances: whether Whig or Republican or Democrat. Yet political parties have shifted over time from progressive to purifier worldviews, and back again. Superficial political labels can often disguise the deeper currents of worldview.

For example, there have been salient occasions in our history when those who followed a purifier current in American worldview suddenly shifted course. The political context of American society can always change, and groups are forced to discard one means— progressive or purifier—to attain their goals. Groups that have been solid purifiers can turn to progressive means. William Lloyd Garrison and the American Peace Society championed pacifism as radical "nonresistance" in the 1850s. They deserted the cause, however, and flocked to the colors in April 1861 when Lincoln called for volunteers. At the annual meeting of the American Peace Society in May, one society member recalled how purifiers at once became progressives:

> The course of the Society, on that occasion, was a surprise to all: a stranger, unapprised of the purpose of the meeting, would have supposed it for the vindication of war, rather than that of peace.[8]

In the 1930s purifiers on the socialist Left vocally denounced isolationism and demanded U.S. involvement against "Fascist aggression" in Abyssinia and Spain. Their "internationalism" ironically encouraged what would become the ultimate expansion of the American progressive mission after 1945. And there were progressives that became purifiers. Those who followed Woodrow Wilson's call and fought with the American Expeditionary Force in France in 1918 later renounced U.S. intervention in European affairs. Many A.E.F. veterans helped to shape the neutrality legislation that marked the high tide of "isolationism."

Purifiers and progressives do not wear neat and correspondent political colors. The Right was a bastion of American antiwar chastity during the era of the Ludlow Amendment, as was the populist Left. Today, extreme right- and left-wing constituencies share an unusual intimacy. Both seek American withdrawal and purification. Libertarians and Unitarians, for example, reflect a curious convergence as they call for strategic withdrawal, disarmament, and social reform.[9]

The apparent irony of this convergence is superficial. Progress and purification are ultimately linked for Americans. They are different means to a common end. The ability of the rigid disciples of radical nonviolence to "lock-and-load" with the Grand Army of the Republic, the readiness of A.E.F. veterans to champion isolation in Congress, evokes the strong if hidden bridge between progress and purification.

The images of "progressive" and "purifier" are intended to evoke two basic and still unresolved paths for an American mission. The tension between them is reflected in a historically confused American approach to national security. Since the end of World War II the United States has maintained a progressive construction of national security. It has been upheld longer than any former expansive interpretation of the American mission. Yet many believe it is eroding. Purifier groups in U.S. society have grown strong in recent years. Although the debate over national security is really a contest between progressive and purifier, between two directions for the American future, the visible issues emerge through slogans like "No More Vietnams" and "No Nukes."

And, now, with "Star Wars."

2.
THE SDI DEBATE AS A LEGACY OF AMERICAN TRADITIONS

The debate over strategic defense—"Star Wars"—is being waged over these fundamental issues: Who are we? Where do we come from? Where are we going?

The voices defending and attacking the Strategic Defense Initiative (SDI) are full of passion. The language may sound like a debate over national security. But the emotions expressed emerge from out of our visions and fears about the American future. We define ourselves in our future. The stress we feel discussing strategic defense is related then to our sense of national identity.

The voices raised for and against strategic defense are descended from earlier progressive and purifier visions of American mission. They seek roots in the world before 1945. They look to an America that linked national-security policy to traditional values. This must be recognized.

The debate over SDI is a reemergence of the passionate over the pragmatic in American national security. Strategic defense implies much more than change in strategic nuclear posture. It is a potential departure by society from a goal of "nuclear stability" to a kind of nuclear disestablishment.

Star Wars supporters are certainly within the progressive tradition. The vision of SDI evokes an earlier age of American manifest destiny. SDI describes a new place for the physical expansion of the United States: "space, the final frontier." SDI renews an American precept lost after 1945: control of our own destiny. The progressive argument reads like this: Nuclear weapons are not the only immorality. It is immoral as well for American citizens to live exposed to destruction. It is wrong to yield their safety to the restraint of a potential enemy.[10]

The Star Wars iconoclasts—those who see SDI as unmitigated immorality—are purifiers. They, too, believe that prevention of nuclear war ultimatley hinges on nuclear disestablishment. But they see SDI as an attempt to substitute other kinds of military force for nuclear deterrence. If successful, this would perpetuate the legitimacy and reality of war. If unsuccessful, they insist, SDI would promote, not prevent, a nuclear war. Finally, SDI threatens the primacy of arms control as the only accepted process to an eventual nuclear disestablishment. Arms control is the only way to control the threat of war. An armed world cannot secure "real peace," with or without nuclear weapons.[11]

However defensive, weapons are still weapons. This has been a tenacious tenet of American purifiers since the beginning. They opposed first the big sailing frigates of 1797 and then the battleships of 1890 or 1935 as contributing to a general world climate of antagonism and confrontation. They insist that limited weapons actually tend to make nuclear war more "thinkable," their way of saying more acceptable, and so, more possible. Nuclear weapons paradoxically are cherished by purifiers. Their natural persistence lends inarguable moral force to the call for disarmament. It is the ultimate "horror of war." SDI is to be especially condemned for both eroding the future moral force of the nuclear threat and for doing this with another weapon.

Ironically, then, although purifier and progressive visions of national direction remain juxtaposed, both groups share the goal of nuclear disestablishment. The progressives have embraced change that will strip nuclear weapons of political and military value. The purifiers seek to imprison nuclear weapons through arms control, which they believe is the first step to a disarmed world. Both worldviews promote old ideas of American mission. Both reject the more classically European policies—in particular, the national-security policies of the past forty years—of the postwar pragmatists.[12]

The pragmatists emerged from the wreckage of traditional American mythology. The received truths of World War II indicted

U.S. policies of the 1930s. American isolation from the world had encouraged evil states to start aggressive wars. Eventually, it led them to attack the United States itself. Pearl Harbor showed brutally that the United States lived in a harsh world. The lesson to both isolationists and internationalists (who in the 1930s sought American involvement in the world without corollary rearmament) was that their prewar policies were foolish and dangerous.[13]

Even in 1945 this lesson was still not fully accepted. Global war seemed to finish the issue of Nazi evil, and the United Nations and great power détente seemed sufficient solution to keep the peace. The hammer blows of Berlin and China and Korea finally drove the lesson home: the world was forever changed, and America's approach to the world must be recast.

The old American traditions of "manifest destiny and mission," in which Yankee forays into the world hewed to an episodic and crusading character, were buried in 1950 by Korea and the cold war. U.S. global responsibilities demanded pragmatic policymaking. The United States, it was said, was a mature great power. It should be guided in the British manner, according to cool and classical calculations of national interest and intervention. The pragmatists sought to "manage" America and the world. They bent their knees to traditional national ideals. But they seemed assured that former notions of national identity would intrude only at the margins of political debate.

Since 1980 all that has changed. Both Left and Right margins unexpectedly unseated the centers of their political parties: they came in from the margins. Pragmatists are now accused of "realism," in tones not dissimilar to epithets of "Old World realpolitik," like Woodrow Wilson's charge against "secret treaties."

The pragmatic center can claim today to have guided the United States through forty years of nuclear peace. The center was shocked then to be judged by purifiers as morally guilty of wishing to perpetuate the nuclear world. It was no longer sufficient to say that peace was possible only through preparation for nuclear war.

The postwar pragmatists have sought to defend their postwar strategic architecture. By their measurement, it has sheltered the liberty of the West and upheld a nuclear peace. Yet change is the core of both progressive and purifier challenges to the pragmatic center. The center in contrast has pushed stability, the opposite of change.

Always, technology is the touchstone of change. Technology is a symbol of the American mission for both progressives and purifiers. For SDI supporters, technology is assurance of achievement. Technology is the sign of America's calling. It is America's special gift. The impact of this nation on world history can be seen through the impact of technology.

For the iconoclasts, technology is in itself suspect. It may even be an agency of evil. A few SDI opponents in the popular press sound like Luddites. They are as full of anger and fear as were their ancestors during the industrial revolution.[14]

Anti–Star Wars diatribes describe SDI as technology "gone mad." SDI becomes a symbol of a larger problem. Technology worship in American society is destroying the environment and dehumanizing Man. SDI symbolizes an unnatural course for Man. Weapons in space, to the extreme purifier are, like the clarion of "Man in space," an image of celestial violation. Although couched in the sober language of pragmatism, the distaste for the physical-heroic in space is ultimately a rejection of the progressive half of the the American ethos.

> The real Niñas and Pintas today are unmanned probes...the most lofty justification for manned space travel is that it satisfies, as all 'Star Trek' fans know, the urge 'to boldly go where no man has gone before.' But a mission to Mars would be timidly revisiting a place we went years ago. As an expression of the human spirit, manned space exploration is rather complacent.... Sally Ride on Mars would be nothing more than a $100 billion flag-planter.[15]

Both progressives and purifiers understand that SDI means change. Progressives would embrace change as relief, even sanctuary from a frightening and uncertain present. Purifiers also fear and loathe the nuclear present. Unrelenting change brought us the dilemmas of the present, and increasing the pace of change can bring only more danger. They want a different kind of change.

To the progressive, technology is the instrument of American destiny: it is what made us and preserved us. It created the hope of a free world. To the purifier, technology has been the instrument corrupting America and endangering the world. To the postwar pragmatists, technology represented a mechanism of balance, the eccentric of a stable-state political universe.

"Technology" for each group is simply a part of the litany of our hope or despair for the future.

By offering a unified national goal, SDI has already linked progressives and purifiers (and transcended the pragmatists). By encapsulating motifs that both visions share, by aspiring to a righteous construction of national security free of the cynicism of nuclear deterrence through threat of annihilation, it might even seem to be a potential means of binding two strands in the American ethos. SDI does not promote an agenda of arms control, however, so it is rejected by the purifiers. SDI is embraced by the progressives, but often for the wrong reasons. It is seen as a national deus ex machina, the intervention of an ancestral, almost godlike instrumentality that will return us to the romantic landscape of security we once enjoyed. SDI is scourged and worshipped, ultimately, for its sense of promise. It is almost instinctively understood by Americans. It resonates to our national hymn.

Because it strikes so deep a chord, SDI represents a potential point of departure from the pragmatists' sense of an American mission. It can overturn the world as it was remade after 1950. But maybe that world is already changed. Maybe SDI only brings the recognition of change. Even its most impassioned critics, stirred up by the Nuclear Freeze, push for a departure, at least from the nuclear world. While purifier and progressive directions for an American character diverge, their goals for Americans somehow merge on the horizon.

The desire for escape from the present nuclear world is in itself important. It implies perhaps a desire for Americans to escape the entire sum of commitments and entanglements snared since the last great war. The promise of SDI, and the ways in which it might change the context of American national security, raise these questions:

- How, after forty years, did the idea of fundamental change become politically legitimate?

- Why the groundswell for nuclear disestablishment,.and how did a yearning for nuclear abolition lead to SDI?

- How did the center, the guiding postwar pragmatists, lose the American consensus?

- How did a president come to inspire a vision for progressives and renounce the status quo of seven predecessors?

Is the vision of SDI a rejection of a "pragmatic" postwar American mission, or is it ultimately a more basic rejection of a national-security doctrine of deterrence rooted in nuclear determinism?

3.
THE CHALLENGE TO NUCLEAR DETERRENCE

Genesis: Change in a Nuclear World

The "nuclear world" as it came to be known after 1945 seemed a new place. All former notions of the uses of military force in international relations were swept away. Everything had changed. The atomic bomb magnified the dynamism of modern strategy, which had been scarred already by city bombing, poison gas, and "total war." The twentieth century was a century of change, change wrought by technology. Nuclear fission was now its most visible symbol. Atomic weapons and their deadly delivery systems multiplied. The "arms race" was reality, bomber and missile "gaps" the perceptual norm. It was frightening. And it was inescapable.

The face of the nuclear world appeared to change in the 1960s. The fear of the threat of nuclear war was assuaged by a national confidence in U.S. nuclear capability. President Kennedy had rekindled faith in American strength; the military buildup of his administration erased the public uncertainties created by bomber and missile gaps.

Moreover, Americans assumed that the technology of nuclear systems had reached an evolutionary plateau and that the U.S. nuclear advantage could, conceivably, be extended forever. It was even said that the Soviets also accepted this notion of a nuclear plateau. They understood that a condition of stability naturally encouraged a "stable nuclear balance." Kremlin leaders, so it was argued, could no longer hope to achieve a nuclear advantage over the United States. Conviction replaced uncertainty as American policymakers came to believe that the United States could control the strategic nuclear balance to its advantage.[16]

World War II had added a leitmotiv to the American mythic symphony. The United States had experienced no national failure after its victory in 1945. Its energies seemed equal to the threat of nuclear war. Kennedy's inaugural charge radiated national confidence. A nuclear world could be harnessed by the United States, just as a turbulent world could be uplifted and an implacable adversary ultimately reformed.

An authentic American school of strategy, nurtured after the war at places like Yale and MIT and Rand, seemed to have grown to maturity. It added to these other strengths. Among its tenets, as announced by secretary of defense Robert McNamara in 1967, was the conviction that Soviet behavior could be conditioned by U.S. actions, just as the United States could control the dynamics of the arms race. These assumptions formed a kind of cultural projection. American policymaking perspectives were pasted onto the adversary to become our understanding of Soviet strategic worldview. It was all too easy to conclude, after assuming they possessed a rational approach to strategy, that the Soviets accepted our tenets of nuclear stability as well.[17]

This new reality was capped by an arms-control policy that tied American military posture to a reform agenda. No longer was Western nuclear capability focused simply on deterrence of war: it existed now to encourage arms limitations. Nuclear forces resembled the Roman god Janus, with one face looking to war, and one to peace. Before, SAC (Strategic Air Command) could say with a straight face that "Peace Is Our Profession." Weapons' existence preserved the peace. Now, the government was implying that only a decline in weapons could be described as promoting peace.[18] Confidence in U.S. nuclear strength, an assumption that the Soviets would not bid for nuclear advantage, and a desire among pragmatists to pursue goals of stability and arms limitation integral to the American tradition led to a promise of change in the nuclear world.

By the 1970s it appeared that the path of stability was fully cleared, if not yet paved. At its policy terminus it offered a seductive vision with strong Early American roots: détente. The "peaceable kingdom" seemed possible. The assumptions of the policymakers of the 1960s had been proved. The nuclear balance remained stabilized. Arms-control agreements were edging toward real arms limitation.

Darker undercurrents, however, were at work, which would erode American confidence in the strategic theories of the 1960s, while at the same time, perversely, strengthen their goals. The pragmatists who shaped these theories framed goals of nuclear stability and arms limitation through a posture of American nuclear strength. The goals were consonant with national core values, but the means to achieve them were borrowed from classical, European strategic tradition.

National failure in Vietnam undermined the policy hold of the pragmatic center and ended in destroying its fragile postwar legitimacy. Ultimately, Vietnam was a failure that penetrated to the core of the pragmatists' strategic premises. Theories implying almost scientific principles were applied in Vietnam. They were devoid of the traditional emotional content of American wars, which focused on a kind of crusading reformation of the enemy. The callous theories of "graduated response" and "escalation control" failed to reinforce the core values of national ethos. Vietnam was not seen as a failure of theories misapplied. The theories themselves, it was said, and those who made them, were wrong.[19] Yet these theories had also been applied wholesale to the doctrine of nuclear deterrence.

National failure in Vietnam led not only to a partial American retreat in the Third World. It also inspired a reemergence of progressive and purifier worldviews. Among Democrats, these had been in uneasy coalition since 1950. Largely as a function of internecine political combat over Vietnam policy, the challenge to pragmatist strategy emerged first in the Democratic party. In the 1972 convention, purifier constituencies seized control of the party. Although ameliorated since, purifier views have remained ascendant among Democrats. Their planks have exalted arms control and détente as a new American strategy, along with a kind of "soft internationalism" as a substitute for containment. This geopolitical vision of containment, created by the Truman progressives of the late 1940s, was in eclipse, labeled as "neo-imperialism."

The Republican pragmatists under Nixon survived a while longer. They sought to limit the damage of American defeat by accommodating the Soviet Union. This was presented for public consumption, however, as a kind of "peace in our time." Intended to buy time for Western recovery, the Nixon course only promoted eventual rebellion among radical and populist Republicans, who saw in accommodation with evil a corruption of American righteousness and, ultimately, of the American mission. To Republican purifiers reminiscent of the old isolationists and Republican progressives driven by a globalist anticommunism, Watergate was the rallying cry for a rejection of the Nixonian pragmatists. This led to Reagan's eventual coup de main.

Nixon's "atmospherics" of arms control and détente, however, publicly altered the image of the adversary in the early 1970s. The Soviets were now mirror-image instead of mirror-opposite. Arms control became a problem of communication, not of ideology. This implied that the weapons themselves were the problem. Real security could be based on mutual understanding. Impending superpower rapprochement made nuclear deterrence based on American strategic advantage look passé. The question that underlay Nixonian détente: "What in the name of God is 'strategic superiority'?"

In this climate of political upheaval, national defeat, and hopeful accommodation with the enemy, an intellectual pressure may have been the most insidious. An academic school of historical "revisionism" poisoned all that was positive in our public myths of the postwar era. The American mission was a sham, revisionists wrote. A strategy of global leadership and containment was retold as a crude kind of nineteenth-century manifest destiny. The revisionists, dominated by purifiers and penitent progressives, called for a return to the spiritual sources of American conduct. In their writings, an American mission informed by the historical "lessons" of global war and prewar appeasement was renounced. Traditional American morality meant abstention from corrupting policies.

The United States had transgressed. It had lost its original sense of purpose. It was now no more than a sordid empire. Since 1945 it had initiated two evil wars against the Third World. It had threatened all Humankind with nuclear holocaust. Historical dispensation required penance. This meant nuclear disarmament, social reform, and good works in the form of alms to the Third World. In this vein, a standard claim was:

> People talk about nuclear weapons as an aberration or something horrible that's just sort of happened. And I think the reality is that nuclear weapons are the dominant force in U.S. foreign policy since 1945, and they've been a major part of the United States dominating the world—economically, socially, and politically.[20]

By the mid-1970s the pragmatic center was under terrific pressure from two traditional directions in the American ethos. A reemergence of purifiers, generally but not wholly identifying themselves on the political Left, pressured the dominant Democratic center during and after the Vietnam War. With the nomination of George McGovern in 1972, the purifier vision, long buried during decades of world wars and cold wars reassumed the mantle of 1932. Pragmatists in the party accommodated the change, attempting after 1976 to pull the Democrats' agenda back to the center. Progressives in the party, the cold warriors of NSC–68 and Korea, fought back, but their last bastion crumbled after the death of Senator Henry Jackson in 1982. Many, like Jeanne Kirkpatrick and Richard Perle, became renegades and joined the newly progressive Republican camp.

Nixon's stigmata of Watergate ultimately impugned the pragmatists in the Grand Old Party. Republican populists under Reagan attacked in 1976 and were narrowly defeated by the Ford coterie. It was a pyrrhic victory for them, however, and by 1980 Reagan's time had come. Although not burdened by direct culpability for Vietnam, as were the Democrat pragmatists, their association with Kissinger and classical grand strategy tainted the pragmatists fatally. It also infected the credibility of their strategic policies. The assumed failure of these policies permitted the Reagan progressives eventually to conjure an alternative in the form of SDI.

But in the later 1970s it was purifier political pressures that burdened both the Ford and Carter administrations. Responding first to the political and military failures of the 1970s, the purifiers eventually came to fasten on the evil of nuclear weapons. This process of political fixation was intensified by the twin failures of arms control and strategic modernization after 1975.

Failure of the Nuclear Elite

The struggle for power within the arms-control community after 1975 can be traced to domestic stresses and to Soviet behavior, which chafed away at pragmatist policies of nuclear deterrence. First, the pragmatists' moderate arms-control strategy had not made the world a safer place. In fact, the world had very quickly become a more dangerous place. The Soviet response to arms control had been to use it to their own advantage: to build up their nuclear forces while holding back U.S. strategic programs. The achievements of early arms-control agreements, especially SALT I, were seen by many as clearly damaging to the U.S. strategic nuclear position. SALT II was merely a protracted attempt to limit its damage. Consequently, internal strife flared up about the utility—even the safety—of arms control as the centerpiece of U.S. strategic policy.[21]

Second, pragmatist efforts at strategic modernization crumbled from public pressures unintentionally created by détente and purifier political lobbies, which slowed attempts to modernize America's aging nuclear arsenal. Even in 1983 enormous political effort was needed to put Intermediate Nuclear Forces (INF) into Western Europe. Finally, strategic modernization failed with its critical capstone: the MX ICBM.

The self-evisceration of the strategic community came at the end of the 1970s with the final collapse of détente. The pragmatic center showed itself incapable of passing SALT II and, then, of getting reelected. It could not achieve its moderate arms-control agenda. With the coming of Reagan, it would not get another chance.

Many pragmatists yielded to the purifiers, abandoning the course of long-term goals through moderate change for the road of rapid and radical solutions. Many from the postwar center converted. The "Gang of Four" was one sharp highlight of pragmatists-turned-purifiers. Within the Republican camp, the pragmatic center had been banished momentarily for abetting the decline of American power. But for this group, the answer was not to be found in a purifier agenda for arms control. Quite the reverse. Strategic pragmatists, like Harry Rowen and Albert Wohlstetter, embraced the progressive worldview and called for a reassertion of U.S. nuclear advantage.

The postwar strength of the pragmatic center, built on the received "truths" of the 1930s and 1940s, was diminished. Its non-partisan political unity—the unity of deterrence—was gone. The margins had conquered the center.

The situation was unusual. Policymaking elites were now visibly dominated by traditional notions of national security. Extreme progressives and purifiers holding media center-stage spoke in lurid language for public consumption. Together, they generated a kind of national-security symbiosis. They needed each other for the consummation of their passion. These voices were comfortable with radical agenda and spectral futures inevitable if prophesy and Cassandra-warning were not heeded.

The result of fear-mongering after 1980 was fear itself. The collapse of détente and civil feuding within the arms-control community inspired real public apprehension. When the Soviet Union rushed to take advantage by stoking the fires of the "Euromissile" crisis, they inflamed only a latent hysteria.

At first startled by the intensity of the nuclear debate, the public began to question the notion of nuclear deterrence. For more than a generation they had accepted the pragmatists' "nuclear reality" and grown accustomed to a certain balance and moderation of tone in elite language describing such policies as "deterrence," "retaliation," and "assured destruction." But the elites had fractured, and public trust drifted. After the failures of the 1970s public confidence in national policy waned. No longer could Americans be consoled or comforted by nuclear deterrence. And in the face of a remorseless Soviet nuclear buildup, postwar strategic theories seemed especially fragile. This time of fear was to have serious cultural consequences; ultimately, it changed the terms of reference for national-security policy.

The Rebellion Against Nuclear Deterrence

American worldview shifted between 1979 and 1983. Not only were popular attitudes transformed but the group agenda of influential social "guilds" changed as well. What had been lost was more than superficial political support for deterrence. It was the confident belief that underlay it: that the best—the only—way to secure the

..ited States from nuclear attack was through the credible threat of nuclear retaliation. Could confidence and security continue if this threat was no longer believed? And if it was believed, but simply wrong, could it be continued?

The change in public perceptions was sensationalized in a spate of television and cinema portrayals of nuclear war. Films of the early 1980s exceeded those popular in the early 1960s; *The Day After, Testament,* and *Threads* attempted an emotional devastation in sharp contrast to *Fail Safe* and *Doctor Strangelove.* Those earlier movies merely looked at how war might start and warned of our inability to control a nuclear "accident."

Today's films, however, focus on war and a postwar world. Unlike *Fail Safe,* they are not sanctimonious. Unlike *Doctor Strangelove,* they dare not risk humor. They are proselytizing films: not political propaganda, but American secular missionary tracts. Their appeal is much like a fire and brimstone sermon, and through fear they seek to convert and reform.[22] Instead of insisting that we vigilantly keep the cork tight on the "nuclear genie," they preach that these weapons will destroy us unless we repent our evil ways and rid ourselves of them soon. These films form the catechism of the purifiers. Their verses read like this:

- Nuclear evil is in the weapons themselves, like a monstrous incubus. We and the Soviets are in their thrall.[9]

- Peace is not the absence of war, but the absence of nuclear weapons. As long as there are nuclear weapons, there will one day be nuclear war. (Of course, one might say that this is implicit in President Reagan's vision as well.)[10]

- Imagined Soviet crimes are less important than nuclear disestablishment. The Soviets are people and can be reformed. The weapons are irreconcilable evil.[11]

- The longer the United States keeps nuclear weapons, the more their evil will enter into us. Absolute weapons corrupt absolutely.[12]

- We created nuclear weapons; we are therefore guilty of a cardinal sin. We must take the first step, and the major risk, to their abolition.[13]

As Jonathan Schell wrote, in *The Abolition*, "Nuclear weapons are truly an evil obsession: they can somehow drag us down even as we try to fight them. They soil us."[23]

Three legitimate groups enshrined these theses: a political coalition for a Nuclear Freeze; the Union of Concerned Scientists and those who have pushed the Nuclear Winter nostrum; and the U.S. Catholic Conference (USCC), which promoted the pastoral letter of American bishops. Seeking to create electoral pressure to achieve radical arms control, these groups have employed many tactics reminiscent of the nineteenth-century abolitionist movement: they have made it politically dangerous, intellectually dangerous, and morally dangerous to defend the status quo.

The Nuclear Freeze tried to create a bandwagon that would be politically dangerous for any officeholder to oppose. The key declaration was that the potential for nuclear war was a function of the size of nuclear stockpiles. The freeze movement tried to force a consensus that equated nuclear armaments to nuclear war. Once this connection was made, it was imagined that anyone so foolish as to support nuclear armaments would by definition be in favor of nuclear war.[24]

Nuclear Winter was to be unopposable because those who asserted it were unimpeachable. The Sagan set sought to manipulate the abject respect most Americans have for their scientists. The "concerned scientists" also tried to make it seem as though all scientists with any principles were with them. "Scientists" would redefine strategic reality. Scientific fiat would deny all forms of nuclear utility. The most limited nuclear war would be impossible if even a small atomic dose could trigger nuclear winter and lead to human extinction. Nuclear weapons might be in the hands of the military, but their value would be negated by a higher consciousness.[25]

The Bishop's Pastoral was embraced by the entire purifier community—even the very secular professional Left. The Pastoral had the virtue of declaring in its highly publicized first draft that national defense through threat of nuclear retaliation was immoral. Anyone defending the theory of deterrence was either a very bad man or a fool. Nuclear disarmament was offered as the only and ultimate solution to the nuclear dilemma. Until nuclear weapons could be abolished, their possession would be acceptable only if assurance was given that they would never be used. Some bishops and USCC leaders even declared that capitulation was preferable to the **threat** of nuclear destruction.[26]

These condemnations indicted postwar strategy and undermined the pragmatic center. The importance of the freeze movement was its ability to ingest what had been the center and to shift the boundary markers of national debate. Nuclear abolition was made the center, and nearly every centrist political group now jumped the bandwagon. In order to seize the center, the freeze and its resolutions were watered down to inoffensiveness, but the terms of reference for nuclear debate nonetheless had been changed. The old center, the strategic worldview of the postwar pragmatists, had been replaced by a purifier vision, however hazy, of nuclear abolition.

Progressives supporting the Reagan administration fulminated against purifier groups. They retained a large, if uneasy, following. The "moral high ground," however, was in the hands of the "abolitionists." By 1983 the purifiers had succeeded in damaging public faith in peace through threat of nuclear retaliation. Deterrence had been informally labeled as MAD: Mutual Assured Destruction. Now there seemed no security in the notion of assured destruction. Four administrations had tried to increase U.S. capacity to respond to the threat of Soviet attack with options other than assured destruction, but options short of MAD sought only to limit damage in the event that basic deterrence failed.

The Reagan administration attempted to extend this set of options in what some called a "prevailing" strategy. This promised limited damage, at least, from the application of the threat of nuclear retaliation. The attempt failed. In fact, it added volatile fuel to the purifier movement. The Reagan nuclear strategy, adamantly resisting the freeze formula, was a ready-made mask for purifier portrayal of progressives as warmongers.

4.
WHAT WAS TO BE DONE?

The pragmatists were innocent of the political need to manipulate a skittish public. They lacked the tools to orchestrate a campaign for public confidence. They were equally incapable of defending their nuclear strategy from an unexpected angle of attack: from former members of their own corps and from legitimate political groups—not just from the margins of the American Left or from Soviet propaganda. Revitalizing the morale of Western strategy was a task beyond pragmatic strategists, whose careers had been spent in the pursuit of the unquestioned premises of their strategic world.

The pragmatists faced seemingly insurmountable obstacles. How could they renew American strength and confidence? Strategic modernization was failing. Arms control had failed. The Western publics were losing faith in basic nuclear deterrence.

In response the pragmatic center tried to reassert a strategic nuclear posture that Americans, allies, and adversary had long believed to be "credible." It was hoped that restoration of U.S. strategic posture might reclaim Western public confidence and encourage a Soviet return to the "arms control table." This notion of credibility reposed in a concept called "extended deterrence." Extended deterrence has been called the existential concept from which all U.S. postwar strategy has been derived. What is extended deterrence, and how was it meant to work?

Denial of Soviet Advantage

From the first threats sounding the cold war, the United States has sought to defend its European and Asian allies by deterring Soviet aggression. As a strategy this has required more than deterring the Soviets, however. It has been equally important to convince nervous allies that the military forces upholding deterrence will **deter**. Yet, neither ally nor adversary believed that U.S. conventional forces in Europe after 1945 were sufficient to deter. Only the threat of U.S. nuclear retaliation against Soviet aggression promised true deterrence.

And where was the balance of the U.S. nuclear arsenal after 1945? Why, in the continental United States. Bombers, and later ballistic missiles, became the postwar bedrock of U.S. national security: bombers and missiles based at home could easily threaten to punish a Soviet attack on America's allies. Furthermore, it was efficient and necessary to base U.S. retaliatory forces in the continental United States, given the expense and the vulnerability of U.S. nuclear forces—such as Thor and Jupiter—based in Europe at the end of the 1950s.

The concept at the core of U.S. strategic doctrine was simple: deterrence was the Soviet belief that nuclear forces based in the United States would be used against the Soviets at some point if they attacked U.S. allies.[27] This was "credibility." It could not be questioned as long as U.S. nuclear forces were visibly superior to Soviet forces. A sense of U.S. nuclear superiority lent confidence to this theoretical ability of the United States to cap a theater conflict. The United States, in other words, could stop a Soviet attack on Europe by threatening to "go one higher," to "up the ante." The classic term for this is "escalation dominance."

The Soviet nuclear buildup of the 1970s, however, created a perception of superpower "parity." Parity is a fine state of affairs for a strictly one-on-one military balance. Equal nuclear forces imply equal deterrence. But this works only to deter attacks on each other. Unfortunately, parity implies a subtle erosion in U.S. escalation control. It became more difficult to imagine an attempted extension of deterrence in the context of a European crisis.[28]

However, it would still be possible in a world of parity to preserve the expectation among our allies, and in the minds of

Soviets, that a European war would escalate to an inevitable strategic exchange. Although not lending the confidence of U.S. nuclear advantage, it would provide a **measure** of extended deterrence.

The goal of U.S. strategic modernization programs in the late 1970s was to deny the Soviet Union the fruits of parity. We did not want them to think that their progress might continue and lead eventually to nuclear superiority. Modernization was to renew our belief in extended deterrence; we meant to convince the Soviets as well as ourselves. For their part, the Soviets designed their big arsenal to isolate a theater war, to serve as a buffer for the conduct of "strategic operations." The Soviet goal was to dissuade the use of U.S. strategic systems.

The Kremlin's hopes for eroding U.S. extended deterrence were rooted in expanding Soviet fields of land-based missiles. The Soviet preference for ICBMs is not capricious. Command and control of an ICBM attack is superior to the management of other delivery systems, and intercontinental ballistic missiles can be ignited, can arc into space, and strike targets ten thousand miles away within minutes.

Thousands of such missile boosters, each carrying up to a dozen independently targeted warheads, to be scattered and sowed on American soil, could destroy a large portion of the U.S. nuclear arsenal. This is a major capability. Politically, it is intended to show that it would be pointless for the United States to try to extend deterrence in an escalating theater conflict.

> [A]bout 80% of the Soviet ready, on-launcher, ICBM inventory of nearly 7,000 warheads, not counting refires, is deployed on the SS-18 and SS-19 missiles which were designed to destroy the ICBM leg of the U.S. Triad.[29]

How would this newfound Soviet nuclear capability work in practice? In the past the United States could threaten the Soviet Union with intercontinental weapons if a theater war became uncontainable. In a context of strategic nuclear parity, it would be very difficult to make that threat with confidence. After all, Soviet ICBMs could respond by striking first, with the potential to destroy prompt U.S. countermilitary nuclear capability altogether. (The Trident D5, in the future, will ensure the United States **some** survivable countermilitary force.)

An imaginary excursion in a world of parity draws out equal uncertainties for both the United States and the Soviet Union. What the Soviets can do to us we can still threaten to do to them. If we might lack confidence in extending nuclear deterrence, so they should distrust their ability to forestall the threat of U.S. deterrence.

The problem with the credibility of extended deterrence does not end, however, with the uncertainties of parity. What if the Soviet Union attained a real advanage in ICBMs? This would amount to an ability to overwhelm the most accurate, prompt, and capable U.S. countermilitary nuclear forces at one blow. Any confidence that a world of parity could offer would be shattered.

From the Soviet point of view, an ICBM advantage would suggest more than military confidence. Real political advantage might result, as American apprehension in extending deterrence would mean its retraction. Soviet strategic confidence would then become strategic leverage.

Confidence might even reach a level of conviction if the Soviets came to believe that the United States not only would not but could not contain a theater war. A world of agreed U.S. ICBM disadvantage would be painful. It would be impossible to threaten Soviet strategic forces with limited options. The Soviets would have the means to destroy promptly all U.S. capacity to do so. Marshal N. Ogarkov, writing in 1985, sounded the newfound strategic confidence of the Soviets in their ICBM arsenal.

> Soviet military doctrine demands not only to defend the country, using massive defense means, but also to strike the enemy and crush him in any possible situations.[30]

Of course, the United States would still be able to threaten Soviet cities and leadership if a NATO war continued, but this would be a futile option. The Soviets, after all, could offer equal response. A U.S. president could be faced with a choice between theater defeat or annihilation—without other options. Moreover, Soviet ICBMs need not be actively employed to fulfill their mission; the threat of their use alone would be enough to deflate the deterrent value of U.S. ICBMs.

Today, the Soviet capability to strike U.S. ICBM fields and nonalert bomber strips is intended to dissuade U.S. strategic nuclear "first use" in the context of preventing a Soviet theater victory. The Soviet ICBM is, like the U.S. strategic force of old, a **political** tool to show confident escalation control. In the words of two Soviet generals,

> Soviet military strategy primarily reflects the political strategy of the Communist Party of the Soviet Union. . . . Only political leadership can determine the scale and consistency of bringing to bear the most powerful means of destruction. . . . Of all factors which affect military strategy, the most important are political factors.[31]

Political goals explain the recent Soviet attempt to abort U.S. theater nuclear reinforcement in NATO. U.S. Pershing and cruise missiles were a very modest addition to local NATO forces. The missiles are vulnerable to Soviet conventional attack in a theater war and are insufficient by themselves to extend deterrence. If they had been blocked, however, the Soviet Union could have announced an American withdrawal of will. The Euromissiles were America's stopgap response to a world of parity. They were to show that the United States was still committed to extended deterrence. They were a symbol of American resolve. Cancelation of the Euromissiles would have made them a symbol of the end of extended deterrence, and it would have strengthened Soviet political leverage over Western Europe.

Strategic modernization, as described by former secretary of defense Harold Brown, was an attempt to reassert extended deterrence. Knowing that only substance, not symbol, would work, he programmed nuclear forces that would create uncertainties in Soviet target planning against U.S. ICBMs. Under Brown's concept, MX deployment was not intended to make U.S. ICBMs invulnerable or to threaten the entire Soviet ICBM force. However, because enough U.S. missiles would survive an attack to derail Soviet war aims, the Soviets would not be able to strike the MX with confidence. Soviet planners would be unable to deter U.S. strategic nuclear response in a theater war. They would find themselves deterred, therefore, at lower levels, thus conceding to the United States the escalation control it assumed in 1945.[32]

The MX deployment envisaged by Brown, however, never saw concrete. The token MX voted by Congress during the Reagan tenure cannot do the job. The so-called Midgetman, or mobile ICBM, highly touted for the role of stand-in, is in equally deep trouble politically. Vulnerable to barrage attacks, Midgetman's lasting utility, let alone its ability to correct Soviet nuclear advantage, is uncertain. More important, it is still an ICBM. A new missile on American soil is unwanted. This is part of the change in the nuclear world.

The Trident D5 submarine-launched ballistic missile has been hailed by some as a working substitute for the ICBM. It can hit Soviet military targets accurately, including ICBMs. The Trident D5 is to be deployed, however, in a limited number of submarines (perhaps two dozen at most), and only about half of these will be on patrol. Furthermore, command and control of prompt, counter-military attacks launched from submarines is more uncertain than is the direction of land-based missiles. Sea-based missiles have served as a strategic reserve, not as a weapon of initial use. Will enough D5s be at sea, available, and under control to be seen as a confident ICBM understudy? Without new ICBMs, and a survivable place to put them, the Soviet path to advantage is clear.

Damage Limitation

A limited ballistic missile defense (colloquially, BMD) could serve in theory as a substitute for strategic modernization. Its primary function would be to deny the Soviets confidence in a war-winning option. BMD could potentially reestablish confidence in U.S. escalation control, which would at one stroke reestablish extended deterrence. An exposed alliance would be less vulnerable to Soviet action or U.S. inaction.

There are a number of reasons why limited ballistic missile defense would seem attractive from the vantage of 1980: BMD could work to subtract from Soviet strike capability, just as strategic modernization would add to our own. A deployment of ICBM defenses could help achieve the original goals of strategic modernization. Defenses, unlike ICBMs, might seem less frightening to nuclear-sensitive publics.

Traditional ground-based BMD, however, is inherently limited. It might be able to cope with single warhead ICBMs; however, multiple warhead missiles could overwhelm land-based intercep-tors. Land-based ICBM interceptors could attack the swarm of Soviet warheads only in their terminal flight stage. In this phase it would be effective against incoming nuclear warheads, where the atmosphere would slow and pick out lighter decoys from heavier warheads. But against thousands of RVs, there would not be enough tine to save the targeted U.S. silos.

Successful terminal defenses would need the help of thousands of ICBM aim points to overload a Soviet strike force with more targets to destroy than they have warheads. Traditional terminal defenses require U.S. ICBMs to be shuttled between fields of empty silos in order to waste the cross-targeting of thousands of Soviet warheads. It was this very notion of an expansion of ballistic missile infrastructure—even if it meant only a proliferation of multiple empty silos—that the American people rejected in 1981.

U.S. defense planners were faced with only one alternative: multiplying the opportunities for shooting down ICBMs. This meant essentially that U.S. defenses would have to intercept Soviet ICBMs at earlier stages of their flight. Ground-based ballistic missile de-fenses are useful, even as a limited defense. The problem is not that such a defense would be limited, but that its limits are inherent-ly predictable. Even with a mix of high-atmosphere and terminal defense missiles, however, there is only the short final phase for interception.[33] The issue, however, is not the imperfection of defenses against ICBMs. It remains the promise of damage limita-tion, if only to our own nuclear forces. Defenses can unseat the fragile calculations and perfect scoring needed for a disarming ICBM strike.

Strategic defenses have been built before, even during the nuclear age. There is plenty of precedent. The Soviets have long believed, and invested, in strategic defenses. However inefficient their effort has appeared to some Western analysts, it is consonant with Soviet strategic doctrine, which seeks to limit damage from attack, even if only at the margins.

The Soviets have continually expanded and upgraded their own defensive ring around Moscow. They believe in its limited utility. The Soviets have exploited the chance to test and experiment with the BMD field allowed under the ABM treaty. Arguably, the treaty has aided the overall Soviet effort in strategic defenses, for it would be possible to plan a "breakout" from the treaty. Stockpiling for this eventuality is a resource issue. A long-term lead preparation would make just such a move possible: the erecting of a crude but quick nationwide ballistic missile defense.

Should the United States seek to justify limited BMD deployment, it could do so on several grounds. First, the ABM treaty was designed with revision in mind, at least in the Soviet mind. The treaty terms have built-in room for modification and could be altered to include mutual ground-based BMD deployments (the only kind known when the treaty was signed) if weapons emerged "based on new physical principles." If mutually agreeable, a limited U.S. BMD deployment could be possible within an arms-control regime.

Second, limited BMD would reinforce, rather than unseat, traditional nuclear strategy. It would not compromise deterrence through threat of mutual annihilation. It would not destroy the political usefulness of extended deterrence. And U.S. nuclear policymakers, a distinct part of the ruling class of postwar pragmatists, are comfortable with defensive systems that conform to their worldview.

But the United States essentially rejected limited, ground-based ballistic missile defenses at the end of the 1960s. We even dismantled the single BMD installation allowed under the ABM treaty after 1975. Why and how could strategic defenses return?

5.
THE RETURN OF BMD

There are two reasons why ballistic missile defenses reemerged in the late 1970s to offer a limited defense option: technological progress and a reversal of political judgment. Combined, these two facts changed the attitudes that, in the 1960s, led to a rejection of BMD.

Ballistic missile defenses originally emerged as a U.S. response to Soviet ICBM buildup. The antiballistic missile was intended to counter the ICBM threat, just as U.S. surface-to-air missiles had made Soviet air-breathing bombers of the 1950s vulnerable. By 1969 the United States could define—if not prove—a defense against the Soviet ICBMs, which also, like jet bombers, had at first seemed invulnerable.

But strategic defenses did not clinch a political leap of faith from Congress as nuclear delivery shifted from bomber to ballistic missile. By signing the ABM treaty, U.S. policymakers reaffirmed their belief in MAD, which demanded invulnerability of strategic systems as well as absolute exposure of U.S. and Soviet societies. Although BMD research was allowed to continue, the treaty killed development of the Safeguard ABM system and essentially buried any hopes of a U.S. ballistic missile defense.

The decision to forgo ABM development was not unduly lamented. Although the United States had managed to fashion a rudimentary defense against Soviet ICBMs, it was still difficult in 1969 to shoot them down. Moreover, the Soviets had already taken countermeasures against potential unrestricted ABM deployment by the United States. By creating their own multiple, independently targeted reentry vehicle (MIRV), they had greatly complicated the task of U.S. defense and doomed the development potential of Safeguard. Consequently, prevailing political opinion judged strategic defenses impossible. Not until the late 1970s would technology begin to change these attitudes.[34]

There were three grounds for the political judgment that scuttled the ABM: An ABM program was expensive. It was also considered unnecessary, as it could be expected to yield only marginal benefits to the U.S. nuclear advantage of the 1960s. Finally, the ABM offered only modest increased security for the U.S. nuclear deterrent. Such small gains were offset by contemporary fears of the ABM's potential for changing the strategic balance. The Soviet Union might gain more than the United States in a full-scale defense program, and they might begin to whittle away U.S. advantage in offensive nuclear forces.

However, by 1980 the strategic equation was uncertain and altered in ways unimagined in 1969. The United States now had the short end of stability. In addition, Soviet strategic defensive programs were beginning to suggest an eventual instability not unlike that which the strategic community, a decade earlier, had feared would result if both sides embarked on strategic defense programs. The Soviets seemed to be gaining an advantage and were beginning to violate the same treaty that was to preserve U.S. advantage. And now only the Soviets were competing. It remained for quiet research programs in the U.S. Department of Defense to explore new technologies, mostly as a hedge against technological breakout by the Soviets at the expiration of the ABM treaty. However, by the end of the 1970s a potential synergy in these technologies appeared to offer a renewed potential for strategic defenses: from space.[35]

Yet, no national-security market existed for the BMD technologies of 1980. There was no political champion, no man on a white horse. Reagan's announcement in 1983 of his intention to pursue SDI demarcated a political and cultural watershed in terms of strategic defenses. In a single televised breath, he took strategic defenses from "black programs" to the glare of public policy. He could risk this in part because BMD technologies in the 1980s have greatly improved on those that the Safeguard system offered in the late 1960s. There have been major developments in potential performance areas:

- It is possible to describe BMD technologies in space. Space-based BMD both complements and extends the closed horizon of terminal, terrestrial defenses. It is now possible to intercept ICBMs at all stages of their flight.

- Killing an ICBM no longer requires a nuclear warhead. The new ways to kill ICBMs—from lasers to particle beams—are exotic and nonnuclear. How can this be bad? Killing nukes with nonnuclear force adroitly sidesteps deep-rooted fears of extending the nuclear arena.

- The "battle management" of defenses during a massive missile attack, a battle of missile against missile that would last only seconds, now appears possible. Huge strides in data processing technology since 1970 mean that the management uncertainties of an earlier era have been narrowed.[36]

- With fifteen years of additional space experience, the United States has the means to put heavy payloads into orbit. Defensive systems in space would need a transport vehicle. The shuttle may be too expensive a truck to put a working BMD system into space, but it is a precursor of future, more efficient vehicles like the heralded "spaceplane."[37]

Limited space defenses are an option now. Performance of systems put in place by the year 2000 can be predicted. Several authorities, never enthusiasts of BMD, have suggested system performance for a "near-term" deployment. Harold Brown has written,

> Against an unresponsive threat, the over-all system could possibly have a 50 percent effectiveness—that is, destroy 50 percent of the offensive force before it reached the terminal defenses. Even claims of 90 percent effectiveness might plausibly be advanced.[38]

Brown does not foresee completion of actual systems until at least the late 1990s. Moreover, he does not believe that during the interim the Soviet threat would remain unresponsive, and he is right. Any conclusions we draw about the effectiveness of our own BMD efforts must take into account the development of Soviet countertechnologies.

However, as a response to Reagan's vision of a "defended world," Brown's comments suggest important changes in the old status quo. Before the Reagan speech, that was a world of increasing Soviet strategic strength, uncertain U.S. response, and domestic disenchantment over deterrence. Projections of even 50 percent effectiveness of nonnuclear systems against Soviet nuclear offensive forces can begin to redefine the nuclear world.

By 1980 the eternal stability of a nuclear balance based solely on offensive systems was in question. As pragmatists agonized over possible destabilizing effects of BMD, the existing nuclear balance was itself threatening to become unstable. The pragmatists might have accepted strategic defenses as a way out of a cultural cul-de-sac. With proper political presentation, strategic defenses might have been deployed as a means to reassert the credibility of U.S. extended deterrence, without necessitating a return to multiple protective shelters for the silos of a new ICBM. But they could not bring themselves to return to an option—strategic defense—that they had rejected with such finality in 1972. The pragmatists, even under domestic political attack, still clung to a national-security doctrine that continued to erode and yet could no longer be shored up with crumbling nuclear mortar.

They refused to see that the prospects for the future might be worse without strategic defenses than with them in a controlled, limited form. Part of the appeal of SDI is a promise that the pragmatic center cannot easily deny. Without popular support for strategic modernization, without the means to halt Soviet nuclear expansion, BMD offers strategic refuge. Limited strategic defenses under an arms-control regime might also rein in rogue Soviet strategic programs, now pushing the threshold of an unratified SALT II spirit.

6.
A PRESIDENT'S VISION

If Reagan had never spoken, perhaps the pragmatic center finally might have cemented its own SDI. But speak he did. The images are worth remembering.

> Up to now we have increasingly based our strategy of deterrence upon the threat of retaliation. But what if free people could live secure in the knowledge that their security did not rest on the threat of instant U.S. retaliation to deter a Soviet attack; that we could intercept and destroy strategic ballistic missiles before they reached our soil or that of our allies. I know this is a formidable task...but is it not worth every investment necessary to free the world from the threat of nuclear war?[39]

It was an authentic presidential dream: "This is not a speech that came up; it was a top down speech...a speech that came from the President's heart."[40]

The language of Reagan's vision of a strategic defense initiative recalled the sonorous cadences of Franklin Delano Roosevelt:

> If those days are not to come to pass—if we are to have a world in which we can breathe freely and live in amity without fear—peace-loving nations must make a concerted effort....[41]

Reagan's speech, like FDR's address in Chicago in 1937, unconsciously shared basic unifying sentiments in the American worldview. Its call was not merely authentic, it was autochthonous, as from the ancient Greek sense of the word: a vision springing from ancestral land.

Reagan is not the first U.S. leader to lament the nuclear predicament and to explore some escape clause. Yet, unlike his predecessors, Reagan lacks the political luxury of simple presidential "dissatisfaction" with the all-or-nothing final option represented in a strategy of deterrence. It has been said that he received a dramatic shock of recognition. When he was taken, before the 1980 election, to the heart of Cheyenne Mountain and briefed on the awful, target-by-target, missile-by-missile truth of the SIOP—the Single Integrated Operational Plan, the final script for full nuclear war—he was stunned. The shock he so visibly revealed, the recognition of the terrible responsibility that would soon be his burden, might be called a prefiguration of tragedy. He just said, "There must be another way."

For former presidents the dilemma must have been easier to digest. The ethical problems associated with a potential failure of deterrence were offset by two powerful, reassuring truths: U.S. nuclear strength (if not advantage) and a generation of popular national-security consensus. Reagan faced not only the possibility of Soviet strategic advantage, a fear to which he was by inclination attuned, but a gathering shift in the worldview of American society.[42]

Reagan faced a far more intractable national-security problem than faced by other postwar presidents, for the need to find a military remedy to strategic fragility was not the whole problem. The Soviet buildup and the postponement of U.S. response were difficulties hardly unique to the Reagan administration and had been held at bay before. The significant change in the problem was the corrosion of confidence in deterrence within American society.

The national consensus sustaining deterrence had been riven: or, more precisely, the higher strategic consensus was split. This was not insignificant. The very underpinning of American grand strategy, the nuclear posture of extended deterrence, had always relied on the unstated but wholesale support of the American people. It was less important that a majority of Americans still supported the U.S. strategic posture than that the vocal lobbying of elites stalled needed nuclear programs. They tore at the cohesion of national will central to deterrence.

This splintering of the basic belief system upholding national-security policy has extended to congressional policymaking. Past presidents have had the comfortable option of throwing up their hands and saying: It's a dirty job to keep the peace with nuclear weapons, but somebody's got to do it. Congressional support would generally be assured. That is no longer true.

Given a strategic balance slowly tilting toward the Soviet Union, the Reagan administration had very little time and very little running room to reestablish a shattered consensus. During his first term, Reagan made statements intended to underscore extended deterrence. These were given as strong signals to the Soviets. They had an unintended but destructive domestic impact. Much public support for strategic modernization trickled away in the ensuing storm of purifier protest.

Domestic alienation aside, the pace of Soviet strategic programs demanded prompt response. A very rough deterrent posture could be maintained for some time. Long-term stability in the nuclear balance, however, could not be assured simply by the Trident D5 missile, the B-1B bomber, and improvements in the command and control of nuclear forces. New ballistic missile defense technologies seemed to promise an escape clause that had eluded former postwar presidents.

But Reagan did not call for a limited BMD deployment. Cultural pressures made limited objectives seem insufficient. The denial of Soviet advantage or a more confident extension of deterrence were hard now to sell. The puzzle facing Reagan was bigger than the familiar charge of deterrent credibility. The very strategic worldview of the American public and policymaking elite seemed to be changing, and the change had an air of permanence. Furthermore, the final extent of potential change could not be gauged.

In 1983 protest over deployment of Pershing and cruise missiles in Europe was still high and freeze sentiment still visible and strong. It was natural to assume rising domestic opposition to the U.S. nuclear posture. The fate of MX seemed murky. The best that could be hoped for was a minimal buy of missiles to be housed in exposed Minuteman silos—a far cry from Brown's original concept. Fifty MX missiles would be a pathetic counter to an approaching Soviet strategic advantage.

SDI, then, emerged from a milieu of cultural pressure, technological possibility, and political opportunity. These were blended in Reagan's own imagery. The president's presentation increased the force of change by giving it two strengths: prominance in national debate and a potential for remaking a national consensus. The defended world envisaged by Reagan is intended to embrace both progressive and purifier manifestos in the nuclear debate.

- It is officially nonnuclear, so it does not perpetuate evil. Indeed, it will eventually "make nuclear weapons obsolete."

- It is defensive and thus builds on American traditions of emphasizing a defensive national security.

- It embraces the postwar construction of the American mission. It seeks to strengthen U.S. alliance commitments by detaching an extension of deterrence to protect friends from inevitable escalation to assured destruction.

Finally, SDI attempts to play upon some received postwar truths, approaches to national defense that Americans understood and fully supported. One of these truths was the defense of American cities and citizens from attack. Only in the 1960s was defense against nuclear attack abandoned, and it was not until the ABM treaty of 1972 that this abdication was made official doctrine. The defense of the American people has always been a major presidential responsibility. In the 1950s, it was declaratory policy. There were many reasons why strategic defense was later dropped. It is important to remember, however, that the Safeguard ABM system was first a city defense. This is, after all, a natural goal.

The reaction to Reagan's vision has been mixed. Purifier groups do not believe that SDI, or Star Wars, as they call it, is a useful way to rebuild an American national-security consensus. Old-line pragmatists also oppose SDI, although they might support a very limited ballistic missile defense. Unfortunately, the pragmatists have been unable to contribute to the debate over strategic defenses. Their position was cemented in the Anti-Ballistic Missile Treaty and the scrapping of both strategic defense and the **idea** behind it.

Strategic defenses, with or without an orbiting component, represent a bridge between the goals of progressives and purifiers. Purifiers cannot openly support defensive weapons, because they are weapons. Only arms control, not more arms, can bring lasting peace. But arms control cannot repress the unconscious appeal of SDI, which is why purifiers continue to attack SDI on the grounds that it cannot "work," and not on the grounds that if it did work, it would be "bad." For the progressives, SDI has become a sounding bell for an almost atavistic retelling of traditional American approaches to security.

Reagan has abetted this gravitation. He has distracted many, and triggered spasmodic enmity among others, with his visionary portrait of SDI: of a world free of nuclear weapons. Yet strategic defenses should not be seen just as a vision. Even in less than total form, it could be a real option. For the past fifteen years the United States has attempted to pursue a national goal of security only by deterring its adversary. Deterrence has become complex, and it is expected to work across a range of threatening situations. But it stands alone. We cannot look elsewhere for protection. Americans chafe at its limits.

While American society has not completely rejected deterrence, we all long for something better. Strategic defenses should not promise the heavens or, rather, an astrodome-like roof against falling stars. Strategic defenses should be viewed within the context of more limited, but still significant national-security objectives. They should address some central policy issues. We should not speak of "perfect defenses" but of the impact of usable, if still imperfect, shielding.

There are three very basic objections to strategic defenses, and these must be faced. They come in the form of three assertions, which together share a common denominator.

- The Reagan vision promises a **defended world**. If this desideratum can never be achieved, what can? What use would strategic defenses be if they could not protect us absolutely? Could limited defenses actually degrade our security?

- Reagan's SDI would mean **"arming the heavens."** By moving the U.S.-Soviet arms competition into space, would not U.S. security be weakened? Would arms competition increase? Would a renewed arms race—in space—increase the risk of a nuclear war?

- How would Americans make **the transition** to a strategic world dominated by defensive systems? Could we do so without the managing hand of arms control? Would the Soviets permit the United States to improve its strategic position, or would the fear of U.S. strategic advantage risk a war?

This is the distilled drift of the arguments against strategic defenses. The common denominator is an implication of the impossibility, or at least the terrible danger, of strategic defenses; that a world without defenses, however unsatisfying, would be acceptable. A world with cosmetic defensive systems, as permitted under the ABM treaty or a new agreement, would be fine. Notions of a world where both sides just build defenses, however, are taboo.

Yet it is important to look critically at just such a future. If changes in the attitudes of American culture demand a forceful look at strategic defenses, then it is important to try to suggest specific ways in which a national-security posture with significant defenses would fulfill a national mandate, however implicit its charter.

If defenses are to satisfy cultural yearnings, they must also satisfy strategic imperatives. A world with defenses must meet basic American national-security interests at least as well as the present, all-offensive nuclear world. To describe a potential future with defenses, it is necessary to respond to the basic triad of arguments against that future. Could it work? Would that future be better or worse? How could it ever come to be?

FUTURE

7.
TO A DEFENDED WORLD?

The concept of a "defended world" has been made the stated goal of national-security policy. The concept is central to the debate over strategic defenses. How well must defenses "work," in terms of mutual strategic perceptions, for Reagan's vision to be achieved? If the efficiency of defenses falls short of complete defense, what does SDI offer that the present framework of deterrence does not?

Some argue that a perfect defense is unnecessary, that SDI "works" if it makes defenses stronger than offenses. The question, it is said, is not whether **any** missile warheads get through in an attack but whether **enough** get through to make an attack worthwhile. If strategic defenses make empty the threat of a nuclear attack as a military option, then the "defense" will dominate the "offense." This situation has been called "defense dominance."

Defense dominance, however, puts in play a process that promises eventually to transform the conceptual foundation of a strategy built on the assurance of nuclear retaliation. Those who attack strategic defense by saying that it will not work are really responding to changes in American attitudes that SDI merely signals—an impending rejection of the "nuclear" component of deterrence strategy. Ultimately, the arguments against the technical viability of defensive systems are linked to a nontechnical conviction that a strategic world shaped by defenses would be more insecure than the MAD world of total vulnerability.

Critics of a future world with strategic defenses tend to level three criticisms of defense dominance as a national strategic goal:

- Would defenses be as **useful** as the weapons we have now?

- Would defenses be more **vulnerable** than what we have now?

- Would the basis of our security become more **uncertain**?

Each of these generic areas of denial also represents a component in the belief system of classical nuclear deterrence. In reviewing the specific critiques of a world with unconstrained defenses, it is best to remember that much of the unstated, or even unconscious, opposition to defenses is to their potential impact on classical nuclear deterrence. Defenses undermine the architecture of the pragmatist's strategic world. But the issue for most Americans is different. It is important that the guiding objectives of national-security policy support national goals and values and not simply the traditions of a strategy of nuclear deterrence.

Defense Utility

> If both the Soviet Union and the United States have similar but limited defenses, the United States might protect more nuclear warheads in a Soviet first strike. But if the United States retaliated, fewer of its warheads would actually reach Soviet targets... than under the current circumstances, because of the Soviet defense system. The net cost of nuclear war to Soviet leaders would thus be reduced, and war would become more thinkable.[43]

The main theme is that defenses undercut the current capability of U.S. nuclear retaliation. It is alleged that strategic defenses would fail to perpetuate the nuclear "exchange ratio" of the status quo. This argument assumes that the goal of defenses should be to increase our ability to strike back with nuclear weapons and not our ability to dissuade the Soviets from thinking about using their weapons against us. It looks to strategic defense to encourage the classical deterrence of retaliation rather than to make retaliation irrelevant.

This focus on retaliation only is the argument's flaw. A Soviet attack on the United States would seek to achieve far more than simply to limit the overall number of U.S. warheads available for retaliation. Soviet strategic theory is more demanding. The Soviets seek to prevent the United States from extending deterrence. Soviet ICBM forces exist to destroy any potential U.S. ability to stop a theater war. That means the ability to erase the **balance** of the U.S. capacity to hit Soviet military forces before it can be used.

A Soviet missile strike on U.S. missiles in a defended future would be less effective than an equivalent strike today. Today, Soviet ICBMs could wipe out U.S. land-based missiles. With defenses, they could not hope to achieve this. But the argument above implies that Soviet defenses in this future world would limit the effects of a knee-jerk U.S. nuclear response as much as U.S. defenses would limit a Soviet attack. That of course would be true. But why respond to a Soviet strike spasmodically? Why not choose a more deliberate, staged response? In a defended future we would have forced the Soviets to expend a very major portion of their accurate, prompt nuclear capability to destroy fewer U.S. missiles than they could today.

U.S. strategic defenses would be integrated with nuclear offensive forces. In a kind of strategic synergy, defenses would serve the vital purpose of actually "drawing down" the critical Soviet trump: its "hard-target kill capability." By forcing the Soviets to expend their precious ICBM killers against U.S. defenses, the Soviet attack would in effect "eat up" much of their offensive arsenal, while many intended targets would survive. Any Soviet ICBM buildup to counter U.S. defenses would put the Soviets in a sterile contest in which they would be at the losing end, not only in monetary but strategic terms. The uncertainty that U.S. defenses would impose on the Soviets would force them to employ disproportionate force to achieve an increasingly limited objective.

The United States would have thousands of remaining weapons to use against the Soviet Union. These would include accurate countermilitary nuclear systems in the form of the Trident D5, which would be limited by Soviet BMD, and bombers and cruise missiles, which would be unaffected by Soviet defenses against ICBMs.

The United States would have more nuclear forces available after a Soviet strike with defenses than it would in the undefended present. The Soviets would have dealt the first blow, only to destroy a portion of the U.S. military targets that such an attack would require for it to be a success. They would have expended many of their missiles for nothing, at least in terms of strategic outcome. After a Soviet strike of relatively limited impact, the United States would then be in a position to strike back at the Soviet Union in different ways.

U.S. nuclear forces riding out the Soviet strike might be most effective against targets other than ICBMs and the other strategic operating forces (SOF). They would be devastating against Soviet OMT (Other Military Targets). These are the stuff of a Soviet offensive into Western Europe...the command posts, airfields, divisional trains: the sinews of the probable cause of war and the direct instruments of Soviet aggression.

And the war would most likely be, as it has promised to be since the late 1940s, a war for Western Europe. Soviet strategic defenses, designed to protect the Russian heartland, would be hardly effective attempting to cover a Soviet military offensive as far away as Germany. If the Soviet attack could not be stopped by conventional means, it would be quite exposed to U.S. theater nuclear counterattack. Against a fully developed Soviet homeland BMD, ballistic missiles in the allied strategic arsenal targeted at Soviet theater forces in Eastern Europe would be striking at the edge of the Soviet central BMD pale. The shape of a continental, ground-based strategic defense system, like one that might be emplaced in Soviet Eurasia, would be effective only at the center of its coverage. Fixed, ground-based sites would have limited range, and from the Soviet Union they would be unable to cover actual front operations. Only mobile BMD sites could actually be used in the theater, in which case they would probably be tailored for theater use only.

In theory, an unsuccessful Soviet attack on U.S.-based strategic forces would only open up a Pandora's box of U.S. theater nuclear use against a Soviet offensive in Europe. Such an attack would ruin Soviet war objectives and in itself could not be cushioned by Soviet continental ballistic missile defenses.

Finally, U.S. offensive nuclear forces could be used to degrade and destroy Soviet strategic defenses. Remaining U.S. ICBMs (and there would be many more of them than after a similar strike today) could be launched en masse to cut a path through the thicket of Soviet air defenses for attacks by U.S. bombers and cruise missiles. These in turn could hit the nodes of a Soviet ground-based BMD network.

By initiating an attack on U.S. central strategic systems, the Soviets would be open to a proportionate (but not spasmodic) counterattack on their remaining strategic systems. These would include Soviet ballistic missile submarines that are vulnerable to U.S. attack boats. The Soviets, having had expended much of their ICBM arsenal, would then face the loss of much of their strategic nuclear reserve.

The United States with limited defenses would therefore have a wider set of **options** in response to Soviet attack than today, when a large proportion of U.S. forces are at immediate risk. The United States would retain sufficient missiles after a Soviet strike so that, when Soviet defenses were degraded in counterattacks, their strategic position would be inferior to ours. There would be no point any longer in threatening U.S. ICBMs. This situation would exist even in a world of equal Soviet defenses, because the side at a disadvantage would be the side that attacked first. In contrast to today, when the first striker would gain the advantage, in a world of equal but limited defenses deterrence would be enhanced.

To summarize, a world of limited U.S. defenses, unlike the present, could achieve these U.S. objectives.

- Deny the current Soviet leverage of SOF numbers by extracting a very high cost in exchange for an efficient blitz of U.S. defenses.

- Deny Soviet theater objectives in a war by destroying OMT, which are critical to realizing these goals.

- Make remaining Soviet SOF useless in terms of promoting their actual strategic objectives. They would be relegated to a strategic reserve.

Ultimately, the **presence** of limited defenses would:

- Create an incentive "to go second," and not first in the use of strategic nuclear weapons, because the second striker (the United States) has both the choice of time and place of response and a relative wealth of weapons to be used in areas that really count in terms of depriving the enemy (the USSR) of its war objectives.

Beyond enhancing deterrence, strategic defenses could begin to shape the strategic environment in ways advantageous to the United States. Defenses would move the Soviets away from the utility of a counterforce strike. The choice of U.S. strategic response with defenses would be more confident—and thus deterrence enhancing—than the bleak options of an offensive-only nuclear world, in which the Soviet Union has the offensive advantage.

Defense Vulnerability

> One of the most dangerous possibilities of all is a situation in which the defenses of each nation are to a significant extent vulnerable to pre-emptive attack by the other side. The argument, here too, is that this situation makes a first strike attractive.[44]

Any space-based weapon that can shoot down a missile from earth is going to be even better against another space weapon. Could a Soviet "architecture" of space weapons wipe out U.S. space defenses at one blow? In the presence of strategic defenses, how would first-strike effectiveness be defined so that it would be attractive enough to be contemplated by the Soviets?

Since the operational demands of a perfect attack would be at least as difficult as the realization of a perfect defense, strategic vulnerability becomes more immediately a function of preemption. The task of preemption would not require an attacker to destroy the opponent's system completely. One scenario implies that it would be necessary for the Soviets only to punch a hole through U.S. orbiting defenses to be successful; another describes the degradation of defenses over time.

Several points may be raised to counter the criticism that the potential for preemption would make strategic defenses unacceptably vulnerable. One may suggest that the economic cost of a preemptive capability would be enormous for the Soviets. Moreover, the fruits of their investment would not be realized immediately, and their offensive counters would be designed to destroy the present U.S. system. It could not confidently be programmed to keep pace with the evolution of U.S. "counter-countermeasures" and a future, tougher U.S. space architecture.[45]

Confidence would be key to a preemptive effort. It would not be enough to lessen the operational problems of executing such a strike: it would be essential to eradicate them. Targeting a U.S. defensive net in space would be a definable problem; it could be calculated in theory. Paper targeting, however, cannot guarantee real kill.

A future in which both Soviet and U.S. weapons are deployed in space must assume the possibility of preemption. Would we orbit a space weapons system **before** counter-countermeasures were developed to protect it against preemptive attack? Even as space weapons developed the capacity for self-defense, the attractiveness of preemption would decline. Even if preemption was momentarily appealing, its opportunity would be fleeting. This would be understood. Consequently, threat of preemption is a weak criticism of SDI. For, even at the apogee of opportunity, when would Soviet confidence be high enough to risk the consequences of even partial failure—which, strategically, would equal complete failure? Perhaps some roughly finished historical guideposts may be of help here.

Technologies of defense and offense tend to develop in parallel. The nineteenth-century "race" between gun and armor and the twentieth-century contest between tank and antitank both point to a similar space weapons' competition between offense and defense. Offense and defense keep a rough equivalence as long as technology is **applied equally**.

(It might be said that nuclear weapons have derailed this equation. But the contested subject is the missile system, not its warhead. The explosive power of the RV is irrelevant. What is relevant is the ability of a defensive system to degrade the delivery of an offensive system. Even with nuclear warheads, this would be a crucial problem in a counterforce strike.)

The very environment of military technology is marked by a dynamic tension between offense and defense. Historically, this has resulted in rough parity. This has been true not just in the tug and pull between specific weapons of offense and defense. It applies as well to architectures of weapons systems.

An example of competing systems is the capital ship concept—whether battleship or aircraft carrier—which implied the complete structure of naval power, from ship systems to logistical support to doctrines of use. The capital ship and its rivals—the torpedo boat in the 1890s, the bomber in the 1930s, and the cruise missile today—have been engaged in a century-long struggle. It has not been resolved finally in favor of the "offensive architecture" (the carrier battle group) or the "defensive architecture" (cruise-missile bearing aircraft, submarines, and fast attack craft).[46]

The impact of "emerging technology" has been central to the balancing of offense against defense. The torpedo boat, for instance, initially had a major impact on the strategic world of the 1890s. For a very short time there was a disruptive oscillation in favor of the offense. Battleships were exposed, and torpedo boats theoretically could approach and fire their deadly fish without paying a dissuasive penalty. This was an identifiable "gap" in the technology of offense and defense. Within a decade, however, torpedo boats faced good passive defenses—torpedo nets and anti-torpedo hull compartments—and even more persuasive active defenses. The quick-firing gun created a multiple-layered envelope of anti-torpedo boat fire from the battleship. And then there was the torpedo-boat destroyer, the new battleship escort, that could hold smaller torpedo craft at bay.

Similarly, in the 1930s, there was an equally ephemeral advantage for bombers over battleships. Then battleships grew thickets of antiaircraft artillery. By the next war, these batteries (at least in the U.S. Navy) could beat off air attacks with ease and at ranges outside of torpedo launch. Torpedo and bomb protection robbed aircraft of the "cheap kill." Finally, battleships brought along their own aircraft protection. The anti-battleship lobby of the interwar era never recognized the aircraft carrier. It insisted that the battleship would fall prey to the land-based bomber. But no battleship at sea was ever sunk by "iron" bombs.

History is important to an examination of defensive space systems because it shows the ways in which culture and its dominant assumptions about reality define strategic choices. The late nineteenth century was dominated by a cult of the offensive, in part because it was a symbolic translation of more encompassing beliefs about human progress itself. To the pundits of that era, the offensive was the more "progressive" form of warfare, the more forward-looking, the portent of "things to come." The battleship was easy prey not for its intrinsic vulnerability, but for its associations of social archaism.

In the culturally determined contest between offense and defense a weapons system labeled as "defensive" was often forced to carry a baggage of parochialism and obsolescence. At the beginning of this century the offensive was a cultural law. The offensive would carry all before it. If it did not, then that was a judgment on the weakness of national will in battle. The doctrines of Foch and DuPique did not allow for defensive warfare. Defenses equaled defeat.[47]

Americans have continued to exalt the offensive through this century. In World War I, U.S. intervention on the Western front was successful where Britain and France had failed. This sense of the power of the offensive was reinforced by U.S. experience in World War II, in which we seemed to sweep all before us. The atomic bomb seemed the capstone of an American equation of the offensive with victory. In contrast, images like the Maginot Line are still used as a metaphor of national defeatism.

To some extent, strategic defenses suffer from the postwar American prejudice against defensive weapons. This prejudice shows in the easy manner with which SDI critics reject defenses with a mixture of condescension (to those who would stoop to such indecisive weapons) and conviction (that modern technology inevitably favors the offensive).

Yet, while assessments that favor the inevitable dominance of offensive weapons may reassure deeper cultural assumptions, they have more often been misleading than correct. History can give no assurance that space weapons would remain intrinsically and inevitably at the mercy of attackers. Rather, the inevitable balance typical of offensive and defensive technologies as they evolve into maturity indicates that any opportunity for a preemptive strike would be as limited as it would be fleeting.

There is a final caution to a conviction of the vulnerability of space systems. The consequences of an attacker's failure to preempt with absolute success would be severe. Failure would result in nothing less than a war in space. As attack and counterattack capabilities develop in sophistication, the opportunity for a "knockout blow" in space will have to be weighed against the penalty for failure.

A preemptive attack on U.S. space systems—which would include national technical means of verification—would imply the possibility of imminent Soviet nuclear attack on the United States and constitute strategic warning for U.S. nuclear forces. This would trigger a U.S. strategic response. U.S. strategic forces on alert would be impossible to preempt. The advantage of a surprise attack on the United States would be lost by the need to attack space systems first.

If a Soviet preemptive strike failed, a prolonged war in space might serve as an extended initial phase of a general war. It would become a period of wrestling for advantage in a remote but decisive arena. The duration and outcome of this phase could not be defined confidently before the war. It even would be possible to imagine a war in space without "de-escalation" to earth.

If the United States lost such a war, and the balance somehow could be returned to a pre-defenses world with Soviet offensive nuclear superiority, then the Soviets indeed would win. There are several reasons, however, why this could not happen. First, the Reagan administration has not offered strategic defenses as a straight exchange for strategic offensive forces. Strategic modernization has continued, at least in terms of new bomber aircraft, cruise missiles, and submarine-launched ballistic missiles. These programs, although unsatisfactory from the standpoint of reasserting U.S. strategic goals in the absence of defenses, at least have arrested the massive, if relative decline vis-à-vis Soviet offensive forces in the 1970s.

There is another reason why it would be unlikely for the Soviet Union to win a war in space on its own terms. A Soviet "victory" in space would be a success only in that it would mean the destruction of U.S. space systems (defensive weapons and command and control satellites). Ground-based defenses on both sides would remain. The loss of U.S. systems in space would be counterbalanced by a comparable loss of Soviet space assets. At most, the mutual loss of space assets would return the world to its current, unsatisfactory nuclear balance, complicated by the remaining presence of ground-based strategic defenses on both sides.

Moreover, the destruction of U.S. and Soviet command and control satellites during a space-only conflict would compound the uncertainty surrounding possible nuclear offensive options. Both sides would be on full alert, but without the means to control an effective attack. This situation would resemble more the situation of the late 1950s, when primitive nuclear command and control capabilities would permit wholesale destruction but not the finessed countermilitary nuclear utility that U.S. and Soviet forces have sought since then. Such an outcome would hardly reconstitute strategic advantage for the Soviet Union.

If mutual U.S. and Soviet space capabilities are projected, it would be impossible to measure prewar advantage with confidence. Preemption demands a very high level of confidence, or the emotional abandon of strategic desperation. Even preemption out of desperation, like the Japanese attack on Pearl Harbor, relied on a high level of confidence.

It is often forgotten that the United States presented Japan in 1941 with a chance to exploit temporary U.S. strategic weakness. The Imperial Navy expected to lose ships, but the U.S. fleet was exposed and half of it had been transferred to the Atlantic. The United States offered Japan a "window" of strategic opportunity. Even major loss by the Japanese carrier striking force could be accepted, for it was assumed that it would be traded for a Japanese victory in the western Pacific and a strategic breathing spell. Japan judged that, while the United States was gathering its naval might, Japan would erect a strategic defensive position so strong that the United States would ultimately bow to a compromise peace rather than risk an assault upon it. Thus, tactical desperation was linked to strategic confidence.

Only a presentation of strategic inequality followed by a confidence in something approaching complete victory can begin to justify the risks of a first strike. Equality of capability tends to immobilize. It denies both the perception of advantage and its confident assertion.

This leads us to the last issue: uncertainty.

Defense Uncertainty

The technological uncertainties of missile defense may lead to strategic uncertainty: with defense there will be more possible outcomes, but fewer certain ones, for a nuclear war.[48]

Defense uncertainty is a double-edged perception. While it may heighten a defender's sense of insecurity, unknown variables will also certainly complicate attempts by an attacker to overcome defenses. A greater range of possible outcomes will tend to immobilize attack planning, for the more potential outcomes there are to a war, the greater is the uncertainty. This sense of strategic unease is said to be an important part of deterrence. In contrast, a single expected outcome should also deter, this time through mutual certainty.

Today, there is a single, "certain" outcome of an assured-destruction nuclear exchange: mutual assured destruction. The certainty of that simple truth has deterred both the United States and the Soviet Union from launching an all-out nuclear attack on each other. The possibility of a limited nuclear war or a nuclear strike confined to a purely military plane, although hard to imagine, can however be planned for and can possess a theoretical utility. It is the uncertainties of actual nuclear use, in contrast to theory, that tend to depreciate the value of actual nuclear use.

In the 1960s it was impossible for the Soviet Union to be sure just how closely an attack of a thousand missiles would approximate calculated performance. How many missiles would reach their targets, and how many targets would be destroyed? Americans could take comfort in Soviet uncertainty. That positive uncertainty, however, diminished in the last decade, as Soviet missile strike capability increased. Continuing missile testing and expanded and refined command and control now permit the Soviets the luxury of a precisely calculated ICBM strike plan. They are even attempting to curb comparable U.S. offensive programs by pursuing strategic defenses in the absence of a competing American effort.

Without BMD, it is becoming increasingly incredible that the West could or would deter the Soviet Union in war by risking its own destruction. Strategic defenses, however, would add a needed layer of strategic uncertainty of outcome. This is one of the positive uncertainties of strategic defenses. SDI critics sometimes argue that the uncertainties of BMD would release the Soviets from the certainty of destruction; that BMD would be useless unless its effectiveness was proven perfect. However, strategic defenses need not meet the demands of deterrence based on mutual certainty. They need only raise sufficient doubts about the likely success of a Soviet attack to achieve deterrence. The question then becomes: How effective must such defenses be to inspire a necessary degree of uncertainty?

Imagine a major Soviet attack on U.S. land-based missiles and other military targets. Which incoming Soviet warheads would hit home in such an attack? Today Soviet planners could be confident of near-total success. What would be the picture against a defended U.S. nuclear force? Surely, against a terminal-only U.S. defensive system, the Soviets could be confident that many of their warheads would be on target. Even if they could not determine which warheads would make it past terminal antimissile interceptors, a successful attack would need only to overload the system. If the defense system could handle 5,000 reentry vehicles, then the Soviets would hit it with 10,000.

A layered defense system could unseat such calculations. Even a defense only 50 percent effective could ensure that **some** targets would have a 90 percent chance of survival. The Soviets might know which of their missiles would be shot down early in a boost-phase intercept and which targets would escape their strike as a result. They have the same kind of ''missile away indicator''—which could be used to keep tabs on surviving rockets—that we do. They could not be sure, however, beyond the boost phase, which missiles would still be untouched by U.S. defenses through all the remaining layers.

Some basic problems would remain in attempting to overcome a layered defense. First, to attempt to penetrate U.S. defenses, a Soviet attack would have to be launched essentially in the form of a stream of missiles. Soviet attack managers would need to split-second stagger the massive salvo **after** determining which warheads were not getting through the initial layer of U.S. defenses. This is an acute problem of timing—of coordinating thousands of missiles.

More daunting than this relatively quantifiable dilemma is the level of uncertainty that Soviet planners would confront when attempting to factor in U.S. strategic defense effectiveness. The need for timely ''trans-attack'' assessment of the performance of U.S. defenses **during the strike** would only compound the problem. Early boost-phase assessment would be possible, with the away missiles still close to home command nets. The tactical picture, however, and Soviet control over their missiles, would decay rapidly in later stages of the attack flight.

Against such uncertainties, the Soviets would face a second major problem: calculating the necessary number of missiles to finesse a successful stream attack. How many ICBMs might be lost in the early stages? How could U.S. defense effectiveness be gauged for the duration of the strike, even through its later stages? When might "trans-attack" assessments begin to break down? To compensate for these uncertainties the Soviets would likely counter with a massive increase in the number of their missiles, and literally thousands of ICBMs would be needed. The costs would be staggering.

Finally, to achieve the prompt objectives of a "decapitating" first strike, the Soviets have to limit the time line of the stream of ICBMs and get the entire attack launched very quickly. To compensate for losses to U.S. defenses during the midcourse of flight, the Soviets would be forced to attempt late-course retargeting of RVs. Pulling off such a move is at least as tricky as the problem many say would be faced by space-based defenses in the first place. In other words, in the presence of defenses, the task of the offense would equal that of the defense, but the offense would have to work with far greater certainty than the defense to achieve a victory. And that certainty would not exist.

Thus, because of inherent uncertainties, limited strategic defenses would rob the Soviets of the confidence to initiate a nuclear exchange. U.S. goals do not demand a perfect system, but Soviet goals do. The objective of limited defenses is simply to negate the ability of the Soviets to plan a successful ICBM strike on their own terms. A Soviet ICBM first strike would fail if it did not achieve a prompt and extremely high level of damage against U.S. military targets, but countermeasures to preserve this capacity in the face of defenses are unsatisfactory. The Soviets can try to overload U.S. defenses, but that would mean many thousands of new Soviet ICBMs. They could focus on a smaller "family" of targets, but that would mean accepting limited objectives. Moreover, the time involved for defense suppression, and the signal it would give of an attack to follow, would undermine any value in a first strike.

Even a full-bore Soviet countermeasures program would not alleviate the disadvantage to the attacker created by ballistic missile defenses. Since 1945 a dynamism of change has been the current in the strategic competition between the United States and the Soviet Union. The Soviets accept this and have tried to channel it to their advantage. For the past two decades, only the Soviet Union has pursued strategic defenses. Renewed U.S. competition in strategic defenses would recreate a balancing tension between offenses and defenses. Concern over an offensive weapons break-out by them would be offset by the chance of a defensive break-out...by us.

Strategic defenses, then, have a political as well as a military goal. Their inner purpose would be to change strategic perceptions, to reshape the premises underlying Soviet strategic planning in ways ultimately favorable to the United States. This goal implies the use of strategic defenses to change the very source of Soviet nuclear doctrine: their own concept of nuclear utility.

Defenses and Nuclear Utility

Ultimately, the utility of nuclear weapons reposes in our certainty of collective belief. Both adversary and ally share the conviction that, under certain circumstances, nuclear weapons could be used. Nuclear utility is a concept with political force not dissimilar to the traditional political content of "power" and "influence" in the relations between states through history.

Belief in the threat of employing nuclear munitions is a political perception, just as in former times political leverage was perceived to repose at some irreducible level in military use. Manipulating this perception is the basis of nuclear utility. The military value of nuclear weapons is forever linked to their political value. The threat of assured destruction, "nuclear suicide," has little credibili-ty. A U.S. assertion to extend deterrence, and a Soviet response to control the threat of such an extension, is another matter. Ex-tended deterrence is not only believed; it is the core of cohesion in the Western alliance.

Both the Soviet Union and the United States believe, for dif-ferent reasons, that nuclear utility exists outside of a condition of strategic parity. Extended deterrence, and its Soviet counter of escalation control, are concepts rooted ultimately in calculations of strategic nuclear advantage. The United States cannot accept nuclear utility in the form of parity for two reasons. First, it demands tacit Soviet cooperation, implying Kremlin submission to the status quo. In effect, parity legitimizes the status quo. The Soviets will not give up their "destiny" so easily. Second, parity demands equal effort on both sides if it is to endure. The Soviet Union, however, continues to seek an overall nuclear advantage.

The Soviets' belief in nuclear utility as nuclear advantage is represented by twenty-five years of deliberate nuclear programming. Their strategic nuclear buildup has sought to create a climate of Soviet dominance through the unquestioned image, and the inevitability, of Soviet **military** dominance. They have actively, even brazenly, tried to impress this image on the collective mind of NATO Europe—an image that U.S. passivity has only enhanced.

The United States can survive this competition and preserve the political utility of extended deterrence by manipulating Soviet political perceptions. U.S. goals must be to deprive the Soviets of a belief in advantage as an attainable political object and to do so within Soviet terms of reference. Western concepts like "parity" and "stability" are self-indulgent and do not exist in the Soviet strategic belief system. SDI, however, has the potential to challenge Soviet confidence in the pursuit of strategic advantage.

U.S. ability to leash the Soviet pursuit of strategic advantage was heavily corroded by 1983, a process that was accelerated by a weakened American national consensus. The Strategic Defense Initiative (which might be called a Strategic Perception Initiative) regained maneuvering room for the United States. The impact of SDI on Soviet nuclear expectations is obvious. "Advantage" now seems to flow from our mere intention to develop space-based defenses. Potential deployment of strategic defenses, therefore, does more than increase Soviet nuclear planning uncertainty. Strategic defenses, perfect or imperfect, shift the strategic terms of reference between the United States and the Soviet Union.

Defense dominance as pure reality is less important than its impact on Soviet strategic worldview. After all, Soviet confidence today centers around ballistic missile strike capabilities, which cannot be "field-tested" anymore than could a space defense system. The axiom that credibility must flow from "proof" is less relevant than what the Soviets believe. A world of increasing emphasis on defense is a world in which ICBMs increasingly lose political value.

Several examples from the recent past demonstrate how perception, rather than proof, upheld deterrence. In the early days of the the nuclear age the United States had few nuclear munitions. Those in arsenal were not combat ready. In addition, the only available delivery vehicle—the B–29/B–50—was vulnerable to Soviet interception. A general war with the Soviet Union in 1948–50 could not have been concluded by U.S. use of nuclear weapons.

In 1948 the U.S. Air Force had only thirty modified B–29s able to deliver nuclear bombs. These were augmented by a refined version, the B–50, and a "handful" of B–36s during that year. In June 1947, there were only thirteen nuclear munitions, and in June 1948, only fifty-two. The Harmon Committee Report of May 12, 1949, was highly ambiguous. It concluded that strategic bombardment of the Soviet Union could result in "temporary" loss of up to 40 percent of Soviet industrial capacity, assuming a 100 percent delivery rate. It "doubted whether strategic bombing by itself would cause a Soviet surrender, or prevent Soviet forces from invading. . . Western Europe, the Middle East, and Asia."[49]

Yet our deterrent was believed.

Strategic perceptions can, of course, work the other way around. When the Soviets debuted their first big bombers "equal" to our own, U.S. policymakers were thrown into a panic. We know now that the ten Bisons in the June 11, 1955, fly past in Moscow were the only members of their species. Hundreds were predicted within the year, but those numbers never materialized. To impress Western spectators, the very few on hand flew broad circles and passed over Red Square again and again. Their mission was accomplished.

Again, with *Sputnik*, the Soviets stole a psychic march on the United States. The United States assumed that it would be exposed to massive Soviet ICBM attack within two or three years. "Missile gap" followed "bomber gap" with successful results for the Soviets. The Soviets deterred with a gaggle of bombers and then a clutch of exposed ICBMs for nearly a decade.[50]

The Western response, as it turned out, was well founded. *Bounder* and *Sputnik* were just symptoms of an eventual Soviet intercontinental delivery capability. The first vehicles were primitive, but the momentum pointed to a changed strategic calculus. For a while, Soviet "spectaculars" were a stand-in for actual military capability that would eventually follow, surely and inevitably, and we knew just as surely that it would. That is why such spectacular demonstrations worked.

Change has been moving below the surface of strategic thought for years. It will be recognized the moment the United States deploys BMD in space and the Soviets counter with their own systems. The age of the ICBM will be over, even while ICBMs remain as part of strategic arsenals for many years. This is not as strange as it may sound. The heyday of the intercontinental bomber ended when the first Rand reports of airfield vulnerability appeared. Bombers looked suddenly obsolete. They have waited at the margins while the ICBM has ruled.[51] Bombers may, in fact, return to some prominence, for a world of strategic defenses would be a world in which other nuclear delivery vehicles might be viewed with more confidence. "Air breathers"—cruise missiles and bombers—could be preferred for the task of nuclear delivery, if they can continue to outfox air defenses.

Under strategic defenses both U.S. and Soviet nuclear doctrines will suffer. The United States will lose the capacity to extend deterrence with ICBMs while the Soviets will lose the promise of controlling that deterrence. Even so, U.S. planners might feel this to be the better bargain for the West.

Strategic defenses will not give us a truly defended world for decades, if ever. Defenses will, however, gradually undermine the political and military centrality of ballistic missiles as these weapons are made increasingly marginal. This might, over time, encourage a distancing from a reliance on nuclear use in war. This would encourage a calculation of military advantage more and more in terms of nonnuclear weapons, which might come to free us ultimately from the equation of national strategy and the threat of nuclear use.

Strategic defenses would not need to prove themselves in battle to begin the shift away from nuclear utility. They would be a signal if nothing else. They would be invested with the cultural aura of a historical "turning point." The act of deployment, given such common, if unstated resonances, should encourage an assumption of **ultimate** credibility. As with earlier, startling landmark systems—the A-bomb, the intercontinental jet bomber, the ICBM—their emplacement would be a demonstration of national will. National will, and its perceptual impact on an adversary, is the true source of national power. Weapons in this context can serve a symbolic role equal to their actual military utility.

It is important to clarify the ambiguity lying between Reagan's vision of a defended world and the consequences of **initially** limited strategic defenses. If a defended world cannot be achieved, then this must be recognized openly. For a while, limited defenses would, by shoring up extended deterrence, actually enhance U.S. nuclear utility. Over time, however, the evolution of defenses would undermine the centrality of nuclear use in both U.S. and Soviet strategic doctrines. This should be the long-term goal of SDI. But the first major barrier along the road to a defended world is the Soviet belief in the dominant utility of the ICBM. Even limited defenses hamstring that utility; that is why early defenses that enhance extended deterrence also help clear the path to a defended world.

The turn to strategic defenses would signal another, more fundamental change. By shifting away from an artificial offense-only strategy, U.S. national security could return to the cultural fold where it belongs. To be sustained, our military posture must hew to core national values, and central to these is the control of our own fate. It is less and less acceptable that our lives should depend on the restraint of an inveterate adversary and on a policy (even if it is primarily symbolic) of mutual assured destruction. Strategic defenses afford America the means both to reassert its position in the military balance and to reassume its traditional identity.

Such a future is compelling; it is a goal worthy of purifiers and progressives alike. Nevertheless, some will continue to argue that strategic defense is the wrong means to the right end. Would a future in which defenses had been achieved, they ask, be worth the risk? If it must involve weapons in space, would "arming the heavens" intensify the U.S.-Soviet military competition? These fears are examined in the next chapter.

8.
ARMING THE HEAVENS

One of the great fears of the purifiers is extension of the "arms race." In their worldview the corruption of nuclear competition has been so far confined to the earth; Star Wars would propel nuclear evil into a still sacrosanct place. For many purifiers the image of "arming the heavens" almost hints of celestial transgression, like a primitive shaman's fear of defying the gods.[52] Even a perfect defense would be terrifying because it would require placing weapons in space—and to purifiers, the more weapons, the greater the chance of war. (It is ironic that proposed defensive weapons would be nonnuclear, while existing offensive weapons transitting the heavens would be multimegaton.) The old-line pragmatists also lament the "militarization of space," saying that it would make vulnerable the command support satellites necessary to an offense-only deterrence strategy.

To maintain the fiction that defensive weapons in space, by their very presence, would increase the potentiality of conflict, one must believe that space is today free of U.S.-Soviet military competition. This implies believing that there are no weapons in orbit and that space is just a "new frontier" and an opportunity for exploring future superpower cooperation à la *Apollo-Soyuz*. But space is already "militarized." The heavens are not seeded with nuclear satellite bombs, and yet the use of space by military services is intense. For both the United States and the Soviet Union space is crucial to peacetime security. It is also central to the successful conduct of war.

It is too late to reject the potential of space for strategic reconnaissance, warning, communications, and battle control. This much is reality. The free use of space offers an open window into adversary activities. Communications satellites can connect military units and groups in a global net.

Thirty years ago the military potential of space was recognized hungrily. Strategists before the age of space imagined how it might be used, how space could become the arena of advantage. "Modern" notions about weapons in space are little different from those of an earlier age.

> The very same weapon systems that are currently being developed were all proposed in a remarkably similar way during the late 1950s and early 1960s. Even the arguments that were used to promote these space weapon proposals are similar.[53]

Technology's limits held back the strategists of space and denied them the fulfillment of their vision. From the 1960s through the late 1970s space was pursued aggressively as an avenue for command, control, and communications, but not as a battleground. Projects, such as NABS (Nuclear-Armed Bombardment System), BAMBI (Ballistic Missile Booster Interceptors), and Dynasoar were all canceled or quietly dropped, if ever seriously considered. For example, the cost of delivering nuclear weapons from a hypersonic spaceplane like Dynasoar was infinitely greater than delivery by ballistic missile. Reconnaissance and communications satellites, in contrast, were more efficient than vulnerable U–2-type aircraft.[54]

Orbital space was never a strategic sanctuary by choice. Harnessing the strategic potential of earth orbit was always desired, but the political attitudes toward space as well as technology thresholds leashed strategic imagination. Today it is no longer mutually advantageous to avoid armaments in space. In contrast, it is possible for both the United States and the Soviet Union to seek advantage in space; even marginal advantage would seem to be decisive.

Americans are awakening to this recognition. Increasing dependence on military instruments already in orbit have made existing space systems critical to the conduct of war. Their loss conceivably could cripple the United States' ability to respond to Soviet offensive operations, both in the theater, and against central U.S. forces.

Allied operations would suffer severely from the loss of the U.S. military satellite system, even in a war with the Soviet Union that did not escalate to nuclear use. The importance of space systems to allied security becomes a critical issue when one reflects on the adversary's lesser dependence: "It is apparent that the United States is more dependent on military satellites to perform important military functions than is the Soviet Union."[55]

The Soviets are far less dependent on military satellites to conduct a war. In a theater war a successful Soviet antisatellite campaign could be decisive. The Soviets could afford losses in their satellite net, but the loss of U.S. command and control, as well as strategic warning, would undermine U.S. capacity to extend deterrence. Futhermore, the Soviets could rebuild their satellite net more easily than the United States. They have multiple launch pads; we don't. They have a stockpile of reliable boosters; we don't. They have a proven capacity for a simultaneous satellite launch; we don't. They have the inestimable luxury of using proven ICBM boosters in the inventory for satellite launches; we don't.

This superiority in space could press Soviet advantage for the remainder of the war. It might not permit the Soviet Union to dictate terms, but it might help the Soviets to persuade the Western alliance that NATO could not prevail. With an antisatellite advantage, the Soviets could gain strategic advantage at the margins in a prewar crisis or during the opening stages of a war. Moreover, the Soviets could do this without resort to the threat of nuclear use. Known U.S. vulnerability in space might promote Soviet political goals in a war.

Space, far from its myth as a sanctuary, is militarized and insecure. Worse than insecure, it is unstable. U.S. orbiting systems are crucial and exposed. They invite Soviet attack in crisis. The Soviets know that such a strike would be an act of war. If taken in the context of a general war-crisis, it would risk an immediate U.S. military response.

Opportunities might outweigh risks to make conflict in space an inevitable part even of a theater war; but if a space combat phase became an orthodoxy of conventional war, it would favor the side with superior space logistics. Allied inability to repair the damage of a Soviet space strike would cripple the command and control of NATO operations and, in effect, consent to overall Soviet advantage in a war. An attack on allied satellites defended by U.S. BMD in space, however, would necessarily limit Soviet opportunity to initiate war on earth prematurely. While such an attack "out of the blue" would be an act of war, the certainty of success would be gone. The lure of a cheap, decisive first blow, the cutting edge of a general attack, would be gone. A protracted combat in space, with an uncertain outcome, might still become a fixture of future war. It would no longer be an attractive first gambit for the Soviets.

There can be no question that the military use of space is vital to both U.S. and Soviet objectives. The United States should not hope, as it has traditionally, to try to contain the potential dangers of this use by means of prior agreement. This artifice has been tried before. Arms agreements made by the United States, however, have been broken by potential adversaries as soon as the original advantage of the agreement was replaced by greater advantage in breaking it. Perhaps the closest historical analogy to weapons in space was the Japanese fortification of their Pacific Mandates—the Gilberts, Carolines, and Marshalls—before World War II. While these areas were demilitarized by treaty in 1922, the treaty proved powerless against their remilitarization in the late 1930s.

Similarly, the United States cannot expect current or contemplated treaties to deter the Soviets from pursuing military advantage in space. For the Soviets, space, like Japan's Pacific atolls, is simply too important to ignore. Their programs seek to exploit space as part of a traditional quest for strategic advantage. The Soviet Union is even fielding its own space shuttle. Their copy is yet another bow to the American style of space logistics.

The Soviet space effort, in its formulation and goals, has been reactive since the United States first began to use space for military purposes. Space achievements are seen as a kind of talisman in the Soviet Union's strategic competition with the United States. If the United States orbits defensive weapons in space, the Soviets cannot be content to counter with ground-based defense-suppression installations alone, no matter how impressive. They will by nature and by doctrine be led into a military posture in space. Their prestige, their protestations of parity with the United States, are theatrically symbolized by their relative equality of achievement in space. It was so with *Sputnik*, the first satellite; with Yuri Gagarin, the first man in space; with *Salyut*, the first space station. It will be so soon with their shuttle copy. It must eventually evolve to Star Wars itself.

Yet, the Soviet effort can be used to reinforce U.S. strategic objectives. Soviet space investment effectively could channel military resources into strategic defense, away from strategic offense. By paralleling U.S. strategic posture, the Soviets would in effect endorse it. If, however, the U.S. program falters, the Soviets could cement the rough foundation of the strategic advantage they possess today.

The Soviet effort in space far exceeds the now wounded U.S. program. Having recognized the advantage to be gained from usable weapons in space, the Soviets are pursuing the full promise of such capabilities. Future war on earth will also be fought in space, whether as a contest between defense and defense suppression or as a sprint to knock down and reconstitute command and control satellites. U.S. ability to defend against a Soviet victory in space will hinge on the decision to defend U.S. space systems. If the United States has not developed even the raw ability to emplace these systems, there will be no decision to make.

Space was defined three decades ago as the future arena of strategic advantage. The active pursuit of advantage was restrained by only economic-technical limitation. It was easy for the United States and Soviet Union to agree to restrain activities that they could not pursue. That phase is over. For Americans, only treaty pretense remains. As Soviet military space efforts expand, maintaining that pretense can only increase strategic risk. In essence, then, there are two futures. One includes weapons capabilities in space by both powers. One exists with only Soviet weapons development beyond the earth.

9.
THE TRANSITION

If strategic advantage came to be sought at the margins of earth orbits, then it would seem imperative for the United States to begin to move toward deploying weapons in space. The Soviets have created a climate of uncertainty by suggesting that they would oppose this move. To help stall the deployment of defensive systems in space, Soviet propaganda has sought to create a fearful specter in the American mind called the "transition."

The "balance of terror" comforts as well as frightens. It is tradition. Americans have lived with the atom bomb, even as they have lived under its shadow. Space weapons equal change. Even though Americans yearn for change in the nuclear world, it is natural also to dread the act of change itself. Americans generally, but purifiers especially, fear that the very act of change may be violent.

Americans' aversion to accepting the notion of a strategic transition flows from an unwillingness to recognize that strategic change has already begun. Yet common Americans have set in motion that strategic shift by calling for change in the nuclear world. Americans must face the inevitability of space as a decisive factor in the strategic balance and that only through space can the defensive structures be realized to alter a world dominated by nuclear offenses. Furthermore, although actions taken in space today could seize strategic advantage going into a war and tip the balance, in years beyond, military space developments could actually stabilize that balance. The problem is that space, or more properly, defensive weapons in space, has not yet been integrated into public notions of the balance of power. Unlike the ICBM, it is still at the margins.

Another perceptual obstacle for Americans is their slowness to accept the Soviet challenge, both in terms of strategic defenses (which they are pursuing furiously) and the command of space. Yet Soviet development of BMD and space weapons cannot be ignored. It is a big part of their strategic planning. Strategic change has neither revised nor reformed the Soviet belief system. Indeed, it is a part of it; the Marxist-Leninist flow of history, of shifting means and inevitable ends, is unchanged. Space, in the Soviet mind, is a blend of opportunity and threat. The Soviets are already committed to the manipulation of space for strategic advantage. They are even more determined to cut a path to space that will give them a competitive edge in war. The same attitude holds true for the development of ground-based ballistic missile defenses, but space remains the arena of fascination and fear for Americans in contemplating a strategic transition. As the focus of SDI, space would become as well the front line of the U.S.-Soviet strategic balance.

Finally, it is essential that Americans cease to hope that arms control can arrest strategic change. It is as useless to believe that the United States could prevent Soviet preparations to put weapons in space as it would be to expect that an agreement could prevent the use of such weapons. Purifiers who would reject these twin realities impose upon arms control an impossible mission. Arms control was natural when both superpowers lacked the technology to put usable weapons in space. Now, that technology is at our fingertips. Furthermore, that technology can also sheath space weapons so that they defy "verification." Moreover, the ability of the Soviets to put weapons in space quickly would make an agreement ineffectual. A treaty would not even buy time for the United States in a crisis.

The public centerpiece of a strategic transition would hinge on the deployment of defensive weapons in space. It is mistaken anxiety, however, for Americans to conclude that U.S. entry into this new arena of competition would be the first step to an inevitable war. Since World War II other strategic shifts have occurred, each with fateful fanfare, and U.S.-Soviet relations, while strained, did not snap.

For example, the Soviets squawked when the United States first put reconnaissance satellites over Soviet territory. Their propaganda chorus against SDI today is reminiscent of the threat barrage of the early 1960s, when the Kennedy administration announced its first satellite program. The Soviets couched their opposition in universal legal terms. Like today, they played to American purifier constituencies.

> We cannot agree with the claim that all observation from space including observation for the purpose of collecting intelligence data is in conformity with international law. . . . The object to which such illegal surveillance is directed constitutes a secret guarded by a sovereign state, and regardless of the means by which such an intrusion is carried out, it is in all cases an intrusion.[56]

Today, Soviet rumblings against defensive weapons in space must contend with the fact that what was vocally denounced in the early 1960s, "spy satellites," seemed equally provocative and destabilizing. Yet they are now a kind of mutual custom. Orbiting surveillance is considered something of a national right. Sovereignty now does not extend infinitely into space. In 1962, however, the Soviet defense of territorial space had been demonstrated in the upper atmosphere when the Soviets intercepted a manned U.S. high-altitude vehicle, a U-2. This might have been made an enforcement precedent for space sovereignty. But there was no substance to Soviet threats, even though the temperature fell to classic cold war lows.

> You do not have 50 and 100 megaton bombs. We have bombs stronger than 100 megatons. We placed Gagarin and Titov in space and we can replace them with other loads that can be directed to any place on earth. [These would be a] sword of Damocles [that would] hang over the heads of the imperialists when they decide the question of whether or not they should unleash war.[57]

Khruschev was grandstanding, not threatening. Perhaps he was attempting to limit the damage done to Soviet *Sputnik*-prestige. However, Khruschev might have chosen to make good on his threats. Why did the Soviet Union in the early 1960s avoid a test of space sovereignty and permit U.S. satellites to roam the Russian skies freely, where U-2s had been righteously struck down? The answer is simple. The Soviets then, and now, want the opportunity to engage space for their own use. They do not want to deny themselves a possible strategic opportunity that might improve even marginally the "correlation of forces."

The Soviets, indeed, are driven to push this competition in part by their own myths and fears about America. Soviets tend to believe in American technological superiority. It is seen as a natural strategic advantage. They must be relentless in their efforts to counterbalance it.

The Soviets' notion of strategic change flows from their historical-religious worldview, which is built on a doctrine of determinism: There are inevitable stages to human development introduced by "revolutions." The structure of their reality accepts the notion of impending change. To Soviet Man, strategic change is inevitable. If this change is to help the big change toward world socialism, then it must be managed properly. It must not be resisted.

The Soviets see space systems and strategic defense today as the trend pointers of a general, continuing, "scientific-technical revolution." They assume that the United States holds the scientific-technical advantage—that Americans have created the momentum for a move to space and that American initiative and skill also will make it a reality. It is understandable then that the response of Soviet military planners should take this form.

> The question of space armaments must be taken seriously, even if some elements of it belong only to the realm of science fiction stories. . . . It must be taken seriously because to an increasing extent these scientific fantasies can be realized. It is only a question of time and money.[58]

By drawing on their dialectic traditions, the Soviets have formulated a satisfying approach to the weapons system contest. The concept of "dialectic negation," as described by Marshal Ogarkov in 1985, forces "changed correlations of new types of weapons."

> The process of dialectic negation in military science continues. At the present time combat equipment. . .has reached such status that constant attention is required to study these new tendencies

and the possible consequences of their development. To ignore these tendencies is dangerous.[59] (Emphasis added)

Soviet strategy is first to negate U.S. progress in space and then to seek a Soviet advantage.

The Soviet Union has weathered several strategic challenges in the past by keeping pace with the iron laws of dialectic negation. As a "progressive state," the Soviet Union declares that it will never cling to obsolete but cherished weapons, as have many societies doomed by history. Soviet confidence in weathering historical change has been buoyed by the success of Soviet strategic programming. Postwar U.S. strategic technology was offset again and again by alert Soviet planning. By the early 1970s Soviet strategists began to express some optimism that they could keep pace with the West and contain the threat.

This attitude is underscored by Marshal Grechko's 1973 declaration.

Certainly the imperialists are not going to undertake a direct military attack.... But they are still counting on achieving military superiority, undermining the foundations of international peace and, at a favorable moment, resolving the international dispute between capitalism and socialism by military means.[60]

This classic summary of the Soviet strategic belief system offers some important insights into why planning groups within the Soviet hierarchy integrate space weapons and strategic defenses into a long-term strategy.

- The Soviets believe that U.S. space weapons, and strategic defenses in general, are not in themselves a preparation for military assault on the Soviet state. Rather, they are part of a strategy of indirection. The goal of the West is the acquisition of strategic advantage in order to coerce the forces of socialism.

- The Soviets see any Western initiative to improve allied strategic position as a form of attack. It is a subtle form of "aggression." Western efforts, however, are just pieces in the mosaic of historic conflict between two systems.

- This theory of Western strategy against the Soviet Union is really a projection of Soviet strategy onto the West.

Not all in the Eastern bloc are so pessimistic about scientific-technical advantage. The Soviets are proud of their tenacity. As Soviet Minister of Defense Marshal Sokolov declared in 1985,

> If the United States commences the militarization of space and thereby undermines the existing military-strategic equilibrium, the Soviet Union will be left with no other choice but to adopt countermeasures to restore the situation.[61]

It is important that Sokolov implies that space weapons are already decisive, for they can "undermine" the strategic balance. If he believes this, then they certainly will work, whether to strengthen deterrence or to limit damage. Yet he has apparently drawn a conclusion of equal importance. Without Soviet counter-measures, he seems to say, space weapons would give the United States a strategic advantage. Conversely, he implies that the impact of space weapons can be canceled by a Soviet response.

Soviet propaganda slated for public consumption in the West is both strident and plaintive, in order to influence targeted political groups better. Private Soviet comments are more restrained. They even show some confidence.

There are grounds for a positive Soviet long-term assessment. First, the scientific-technical revolution has forced major revisions in Soviet postwar strategic doctrine. Stalin was fond of "permanent-ly operating factors." This was a notion "which rejected the idea that nuclear weapons had revolutionized warfare and which emphasized a mobilization model of future wars." This was thrown right out in the wake of de-Stalinization, as the Soviets adopted the concept of an all-nuclear war. This approach seemed in sync with the scientific-technical revolution. But this, too, was scrapped for the more contemporary concept of "military potential." This strategic path combines forces in being and mobilization potential.[62]

The Soviet penchant for revisions in strategic doctrine supports the Soviets' belief that change is inevitable. Change may not always be pleasant. It may even lead to temporary shifts in the "correlation of forces." These shifts may even be dangerous. A new strategic world emphasizing defenses and space weapons is not to be rejected out of fear of change. However, the dynamics of change should be controlled.

The second basis for Soviet confidence is the relative equality in U.S.-Soviet space capabilities. The Soviet shuttle copy will make Soviet space logistics more flexible. New heavy-lift boosters will increase Soviet ability to put many weapons into space quickly. Furthermore, Soviet research in some weapon and sensor technologies dwarfs U.S. efforts. The Soviets have shown that they can put space weapons into orbit. A Soviet ballistic missile defense in space is not required if the Kremlin's immediate goal is simply to counter rather than mirror U.S. space-based defenses. Morever, Soviet strategic worldview champions defense. Strategic defenses and defense suppression can be employed effectively from ground bases.[63]

Finally, the Soviets may feel confident about their ability to negate U.S. space efforts because they will have time to respond. The United States will not be able to field a space defense system for at least several years. Soviet planners admit that a mature U.S. space defense network is years away.

> [T]he first generation of space- and ground-based lasers, particle beams, and high-power microwave weapons is likely to appear in the late nineties or at the turn of the century.[64]

Like the United States, the Soviets also can get by in the near term with countermeasures. These will give the existing Soviet offensive arsenal a temporary buffer against SDI. There are several available countermeasures. The Soviets could:

- Multiply the number of intercontinental ballistic missiles. For a time, this counter might appear able to saturate America's first, primitive defense system.

- Begin to deemphasize the primacy of the ICBM and build more bombers and cruise missiles.

- Build big, ground-based laser facilities to shoot down satellites in low-earth orbit.

- Deploy their own orbiting satellite killers.

Soviets believe that they can escape the worst consequences of SDI. They believe that any military-technical advantage is fleeting and that, as long as they can compete, they can rebuild their position. The Soviets will use all tactics possible to slow U.S. space and strategic defense programs. They can, at the very least, shorten the tenure of a U.S. advantage in space. Their hopes go beyond this, however: perhaps they might even forestall the problem of U.S. advantage; if they are very lucky, they might even reverse the trend.

That is why it is so important to the Soviets to slow down SDI.

> Moscow would clearly prefer to stave off an intense U.S. effort to achieve enhanced strategic defense.... Current Soviet defense efforts provide the basis for deployments of ABM and ATBM systems in the future.... Rather than an overt defensive arms race, Moscow would prefer the current limited competition which provides room for "ambiguous" deployments such as the new phased-array radar in Siberia. Moscow would undoubtedly prefer to hold off a competition in defensive technologies until at least the 1990's when its current modernization effort would be completed and ongoing programs more developed.[65]

Soviet belief in a scientific-technical revolution implies commitment not only to its potential but to its inevitable arrival. The Soviets' belief system, as well as their military programs, is adjusting to strategic change.

How will the United States deploy space defenses in the face of Soviet antisatellite programs and efforts to manipulate American fears? The United States must put up the first defensive system in space, and yet this is its biggest problem. It requires more than the flamboyance of a space shuttle. It demands more even than a LOX (liquid oxygen) shuttle. A space logistics vehicle is needed that can quickly throw defensive payloads into space. One of the most critical issues of the transition is the actual moment of deployment by the United States. It will be a moment long awaited. Before the actual launching of systems into space, there would be months, even years, of expectation. It will be an action that cannot afford to fail.

The Soviets will exploit American domestic fears that such a deployment may lead to confrontation. The Soviets will threaten. Even, as in the early 1960s when, far from following on their threats, the Soviets followed our lead instead, many will insist that deployment will mean war.

How can policymakers reassure the American public that the Soviets would be disinclined to act on threat? The United States must be able to present an initial system that could be put up in its entirety, quickly, and be able to defend itself. There must be no easy Soviet **political** suppression of the first stage. Without the obvious option of a relatively low-risk shoot down of the U.S. system, the Soviets would be dissuaded from risking the higher gamble: to initiate full-scale war to prevent deployment. Equally important, Americans would be more inclined to believe that the Soviets would not take such a risk. One way to ensure this would be for the United States to precede any space systems with a ground-based BMD.

Initially ground-based BMD would mean that the strategic equation would already be altered when the first space payloads went up. The public frame of reference for strategic defenses would be changed. Defenses would be a fait accompli, legitimized by the initial ground-based tier. Ground defenses are inherently dual capable: they can help actually to defend U.S. early space systems and, as ground ASATs, shield a U.S. move to space and deter any Soviet thoughts of preemption. It is popular to say that the Soviets cannot pull off a working Red SDI. If they try, we can always counter. However, it is said that if the United States pursues its own SDI, the Soviets will feel threatened. They will not permit us to deploy space-based defenses. Anxious voices warn that it would be dangerous to the point of folly to even consider deployment in the face of Soviet threats.

So arms control is offered as the answer. To those who would end the issue of strategic defenses by recapping them à la 1972, the limitations of arms control must be accepted. It is an insistent fixture on the American cultural landscape, although its major limits are often unstated or ignored.

- Arms control tends to put an artificial ceiling on current programs. Historically, this has worked against the U.S. strategic position. Whether in the Washington treaties of 1922 or the SALT treaties of the 1970s, arms agreements essentially codified U.S. strategic **dis**advantage.

- Arms control is not capable of managing a strategic "transition," especially a displacement that would inevitably be seen as disadvantaging the Soviets. Transitions have a dynamic momentum of their own, which arms-control agreements have attempted to brake but have never harnessed. The best way to "manage" the mutual introduction of strategic defenses may be to use the momentum accumulated toward eventual deployment to pull the Soviets along; they really need little encouragement. The recent Soviet offer of a fifteen-year moratorium on BMD deployment indicates that the Soviets have accepted the reality of U.S. BMD and that arms control for them can restrain development only at the margins.

- There remains a basic contradiction between U.S. arms-control posture and the future viability of our doctrine of nuclear deterrence. Arms-control agreements that only formalize U.S. strategic disadvantage undermine the credibility of deterrence at some levels. If deterrence is rooted in parity (or mutual nonadvantage), then U.S. disadvantage legitimized through agreement signals to the Soviets that we both accept that disadvantage and agree to preserve it. Strategic inequity, then, becomes the legal norm of the strategic balance. (This was the obstacle faced by the Reagan administration when it attempted a corrective strategic buildup.)

These arms-control "truths" imply that a renewed round of strategic competition is inevitable. Indeed, it is going on right now, although the premise that arms control can control that competition stubbornly denies it. Such a competition, openly confronted, can be beneficial rather than disastrous. Analogous contexts from history show this. It is only when one side refuses the challenge or submits that disaster strikes. Charles Fairbanks reminds us that "we must realize that it is quite possible to gain a lasting advantage by increasing one's armaments. Such efforts are not necessarily countered by the other side, and if there is a response it usually does not offset the original action. In fact, the majority of major arms increases have resulted in substantial shifts in the military balance—shifts that endured for a significant period."[66]

U.S. inaction in space will only encourage the Soviet pursuit of advantage in the strategic balance. Once Americans realize that space offers a strategic opportunity—to discourage through defenses the wider Soviet search for advantage—the goal will be to get working systems into orbit. It will not matter, as with the early ballistic missiles, whether or not they work perfectly.

> We are in a strategic space race with the Russians and we have been losing.... Control of space will be decided in the next decade. If the Soviets control space they can control the earth, as in past centuries the nations that controlled the seas dominated the continents.[67]

John F. Kennedy used these images a quarter of a century ago in a way that implied a common American understanding of both the dynamism of the strategic competition with the Soviet Union and its imminent extension to space.

But, twenty-five years later, the command of space is still an alien concept to Americans. The wording itself may seem atavistic, like Alfred Thayer Mahan's "He who commands the sea commands the world," an almost nineteenth-century metaphor from another age. It should be possible to imagine that space "architectures," like fleets of battleships or fields of ICBMs, could come to be linked explicitly to the *rayonnement*—the real but almost indefinable aura— of national power and influence. In this sense, there would be compelling cultural reasons for Soviet acquiescence to a U.S. space weapons deployment. Acceptance would be inevitable, a function of an ironclad scientific-technical revolution. The United States could make it work and, therefore, create a new benchmark of strategic advantage.

As demanded by their own worldview, it would be necessary for the Soviets to compete in space if they hoped to compete as well in the larger arena of national and ideological struggle. The Soviets describe a long-term, almost institutionalized competition. They interpret the search for advantage in space as a straightforward extrapolation of present dynamics and not in terms of a culmination—the moment of crisis. What is happening now is to them a technology-driven process, historically determined. Therefore, even if the United States chooses not to compete in space, the Soviets must, and will.

10.
AFTER THE FACT

For most Americans, especially American strategists, the future is generally assumed to be an extension of the present. It is difficult to imagine radical change, and truly radical change rarely happens quickly. In history, change is gradual, and this permits individuals to hold on more easily to the notion of a status quo. Certainly strategic defenses, if deployed, would promote gradual change in the nuclear world. Their influence on the shape of the future may appear limited to today's generation of leaders, whose sense of the status quo reaches back to the 1950s. Their strategic world may hold its continuity for years. But those growing up today may live to see a future far different, and it is possible that strategic defenses may be at the center of change. Such a future, far away though it may be, should be explored; and it is a future that will begin when strategic defenses are deployed by the United States.

This future is scoffed at by strategists of the pragmatic center, who believe in the sway of the undefended present; excoriated by purifiers, who demand change while dreading its consequences; and shunned by some progressives, who fear that limited ballistic missile defenses that reinforce extended deterrence will cancel attainment of a defended world.

A future in which there are defenses—in which they are evolving, deployed in space, and accepted by both sides without crisis may indeed be unlikely. There are many obstacles to this future. The American domestic political climate may turn against strategic defenses. The technologies of space defenses may not mature. The costs of a working multilayered defense may not pass congressional muster. The Soviets may yet make an arms-control offer we can't (in popular parlance) refuse.

But what if deployment is decided and the weapons go up? It has been argued here that the United States can indeed put defensive "things" into space without proving that they are 100 percent and that it can do so without provoking a war. In other words, a future with space defenses may not be likely, and it is certainly a future that many do not like, but it is possible.

How would the strategic world of that future be described? How would it work? How would a military balance with defenses be weighed? How would superpower competition be conducted with defenses? Would defenses change the calculation of war's risk and war's opportunity?

Defining Strategic Advantage

The most visible change in a world of strategic defenses would come in the way we define the strategic balance. ICBMs, today's measure of advantage, could begin to lose their value the moment defensive weapons are put in space. Early space weapons would be primitive, however, and decades would pass before the ICBM became vestigial. This could happen only when a mature space architecture existed, thirty or more years from now. By then, ballistic missiles would have real utility only after a war in space. War in space would be necessarily limited, with the winning side achieving not total victory but the bargaining position that would come with the seizure of advantage. Calculations of the strategic balance would focus increasingly on the issue of space advantage. Outcomes over a battle between defenses would become the focus of the superpower competition.

Ballistic missiles would be relegated gradually to a status of strategic secure reserve. For many decades they would be able to threaten assured destruction. The use of ballistic missiles in their premier role against enemy strategic forces, however, would be lost. Under only one condition might this traditional role return. Both U.S. and Soviet defensive forces would have to be destroyed, or nearly so. If one side prevailed in space, however, the loser would be so disadvantaged that a return to pre-SDI nuclear strategy would be unthinkable.

In the future, planning for such a war would resemble classical, pre-nuclear strategy. War over space would become the decisive as well as the initial phase of a war. The loser in space would be heavily disadvantaged. This would be the prevailing prewar perception. A war in space, however, offers an advantage as additional escalation break, not unlike that envisaged originally for "flexible response." Essentially, war in space would precede escalation to nuclear use. A war in space would consist of a battle between two defensive architectures and include the issue of survival of orbiting command and control networks. Robust space-earth defenses would resist an easy knockout blow, implying a protracted conflict. If war had also erupted on earth, any escalation to nuclear exchange, theater or strategic, would be restrained until the outcome of the space battle. During a battle over both defenses and command and control, neither side would wish to risk nuclear escalation. There would be both the potential for extended conventional operations and an equally attenuated period for negotiation.

Yet the major war effort in a future with space defenses would be the battle over space. If defenses were cost-effective but their vulnerability was uncertain, the strategic war would focus on defense suppression rather than on the traditional "exchange" of ICBMs. Traditional nuclear forces would become the trump for late-war bargaining. After the battle over space, secure nuclear forces, like the Trident II submarine-launched ballistic missile, would be employed as America's central strategic reserve. ICBMs would be the Soviets' choice. Given the likely attrition suffered by defenses in the space battle, nuclear weapons would still be capable of invoking assured destruction. The loser would be disadvantaged but safe from the threat of surrender to unconditional terms. A war in space might result in sufficient disadvantage to one side to force a compromise peace, but it would be a limited outcome, with concessions only at the margins of both Soviet and American national power.

War on Earth

Since the onset of the cold war NATO has deterred Soviet military strength in tanks and men with nuclear weapons. The simple theory of theater deterrence threatened nuclear use if a Soviet invasion of West Germany could not be contained by conventional means. NATO declared that it would if necessary use nuclear weapons first, and use them early. "Early first use" was effective political cement for an alliance faced for thirty years by the looming shadow of an awesome Soviet military machine.

A general Western disaffection with a doctrine of nuclear deterrence that promised the destruction of Europe to save it has led to elegant, if fragile, doctrines of "conventional deterrence." As currently suggested, these are really no more than pious hopes that NATO might be able to detach itself from spending only a bit more on military forces. The Soviet theater nuclear buildup of the 1980s and the skinflint nature of West European military budgets gives the lie to reliance on conventional deterrence. Ultimately, NATO still pins its survival on the threat of nuclear first use.

Yet, European antinuclear movements rebel against the very underpinnings of NATO security, the almost existential postulates of defense through nuclear deterrence. These antinuclear offspring of deterrence, like their American cousins, represent a rebellion that promises to undermine that doctrine. Can defenses against missiles work to replace an increasingly unworkable political doctrine of NATO nuclear use by reinforcing more traditional forms of military deterrence?

Today it is easy to lob nuclear munitions all over Europe. A cornucopia of theater nuclear systems on both sides is waiting to be served, from artillery to rockets to tactical ballistic missiles to aircraft bombs and missiles. If confidence in their easy delivery was canceled, one might argue, then a powerful threshold against nuclear escalation in a European war would be implanted. A mix of superior antiaircraft and antitactical ballistic missile defenses on the ground and in space might compromise the utility of theater nuclear escalation in future war. As defenses matured, only stealthy aircraft and cruise missiles would be believed able to deliver nuclear weapons in the early stages of a war. This would mean that the most advanced attack technologies of the future might permit the delivery of munitions even in a heavy-defenses battle environment. Therefore, theater nuclear use would be possible in a heavy-defenses environment. Even tactical ballistic missiles would be usable for a time. Both the United States and the Soviet Union would remain somewhat vulnerable to submarine-launched cruise missiles.

But there would be an extra restraint to nuclear use in war. Today, that restraint is a function of the horror and self-defeating potential of nuclear initiation. Tomorrow, in a world of effective defenses, nuclear use might actually be seen to have little **military impact** on the outcome of war operations. Air-launched cruise missiles and "stealth" bombers would be vulnerable to air defenses. Submarine-launched cruise missiles would be vulnerable to antisubmarine defenses in local oceans. Cruise missile submarines would be forced to enter enemy territorial seas to get within range (until such time as 5,000-km. cruise missiles are developed). Submarines would face dense local antisubmarine defenses just as "air breathers" would face an air defense thicket.

The utility of nuclear weapons would then be under pressure from two directions. Strategic defenses would slash their value from on high. Precision nonnuclear munitions would undercut them from below. This process of "conventionalization" in the European theater is already under way. It presents some European analogues to the emergence of SDI in the United States. The search for a viable conventional defense of Europe, like SDI, is a response to change in the nuclear world. Cultural change demands freedom from nuclear dependence while promoting technological alternatives to achieve this goal. SDI can be seen as another path away from nuclear use, responding to a broader process of change in the West.

A major criticism of SDI is that is does not address the **real** problem in NATO security: the conventional balance in central Europe. But defenses, whether space-based or earthbound, help to undercut the utility of the threat of nuclear use. Like defenses, munitions' technology is also aiding in this trend by erasing traditional notions of "nuclear" and "conventional" weapons.

This technology offers the promise of substituting conventional or ambiguous, semi-conventional weapons for tactical nuclear weapons. Why put a nuclear warhead on a cruise missile when a "smart" warhead can do the same job? Or why not replace a 20- or 50-kiloton nuclear warhead with one just big enough for the job? A .01-kiloton warhead would be equivalent to 20,000 pounds of TNT. The British "Grand Slam" deep-penetration bombs of World War II were roughly the same yield. Powerful and accurate munitions, shorn of the horror of indiscriminate destruction, could achieve essential military objectives without the emotional trappings of nuclear invocation. These would be usable—not suicide— weapons, and they might just stop a Soviet offensive in conjunction with theater defenses that would negate the military utility of a Soviet nuclear escalation.

The threat to European cities from large Soviet "tactical" nuclear munitions would remain. Brutal use of these weapons against civilian populations would be their only efficient role. They would become the theater analogues to ballistic missiles in a world dominated by defenses: to be a strategic reserve, an assured destruction bargaining chip.

A European conjunction of SDI and so-called "emerging technologies" have the potential to unseat the old calculations of theater wars, with their attendant "firebreaks" and "escalation ladders." The old and now unsettling chain of escalation to nuclear use in a European war would be broken. With reduced utility of nuclear weapons on a European battlefield, the prospect of a protracted conventional war would be reinforced. Antitactical missiles and precision, or "smart" munitions, however, would give the West a chance of stalemating such a war: Antitactical missiles would reduce the potential of a sudden nuclear strike to resolve the battle in Soviet favor. Highly accurate NATO munitions would tend to blunt the tank-artillery advantage that the Soviets have enjoyed since 1945 on the German plain. Together, they would shape a battlefield no longer congenial to a classical combination of panzers on one hand and theater nukes on the other. It would rob the Soviets of confidence in their carefully planned "strategic operations."

A mature architecture of space defenses, several decades from now, would limit the activity of aircraft from space. Ever-denser ground-based air defenses would only compound the problem for fliers. Relatively small unmanned aircraft, such as cruise missiles, might survive. But the potential to hit tactical aircraft, ships, or even moving ground vehicles would change the very nature of "old" war. Space weapons might be inefficient in this role, but they could still have a big impact.

Many terrestrial targets are vulnerable to an "effectiveness kill." The sensors of ships are fragile things. They cannot be armored or buried deep in a steel hull. Today, they can be knocked out by the electromagnetic pulse of nuclear bursts. Tomorrow, space lasers could blind warships, leaving them wallowing prey for waiting submarines and their long-range cruise missiles. Of course, space lasers could also shield ships. Operations in air and on sea, already dependent on space systems, eventually could be incapable without them.

Defenses and Grand Strategy

Will classic images of geopolitics—in which the very notion of grand strategy is rooted to a terrestrial stage—be changed by a quest for the command of space? Concepts of theater advantage may begin to be linked, as they have been in the age of strategic nuclear delivery, to operations in space. The possibility of a war in space, therefore, could alter subtly traditional grand strategy.

Strategic outflanking, encirclement, and extended fronts, for example, could become aging icons dependent upon advantage in space. If space systems eventually influence classical, "old" war, then notions of strategic position would change. If air and sea and even ground targets could be hit from space, the outcome of theater war would be tied to war in space. The ancient emphasis on the vantage of terrain, the earthly "high ground," would be superceded on high from the heavens.

"Low-intensity conflict," however, should remain untouched by space. Small conflicts in the Third World are already detached from strategic war. For states without space weapons there would be only small wars. Space weapons would in this sense only reinforce the U.S.-Soviet military sway that began with the nuclear world. Naked under the gaze of space systems, other states would be able to use force against the United States or the Soviet Union only at the military margins. Even in the absence of space weapons that can strike the earth, the all-seeing eyes of U.S. and Soviet sensors—backed by overwhelming force—has forced small nation military action into the realm of insurgency and terrorism. For the two great powers, such shadow wars would continue to be an arena of competition completely removed from the influence of space and so from "strategic war."

But the importance of low-intensity conflict would grow. The spreading cities and slums of the Third World are the new centers of global population. Orbiting weapons could have only very limited leverage over dense urban landscapes, where populations can burrow in impenetrable concrete warrens. City combat may in future be the center of Third World resistance to U.S. or Soviet pressure. Beirut, the cockpit of the battle over Lebanon, is just a symptom of a shift in the enactment of Third World battles, in which both Americans and Soviets can intervene only at their peril and on no better than even terms with warring parties. High technology, even at its celestial highest, should continue to have its limits.

Perhaps it might be suggested that the phrase, low-intensity conflict, is itself an indication of strategic change. These gritty wars would be fought at the margins, in "gray areas" below the threshold of major escalatory threat. Unlike general war, which, even in a limited theater war, is believed to be uncontainable and inherently unlimited, low-intensity conflict can be managed. It is safe, and yet it is still possible to play for high political stakes. Both great powers continue to jockey for power in the Third World because they believe that the outcome of gray-area wars can still shift the balance between two sparring systems.

Is there a way to confine strategic competition to the margins?

Defenses and American Strategy

Strategic defenses will enlarge the arena of U.S.-Soviet competition. Orbiting defenses will also make space a new arena of national experience. A defensive architecture in space will intensify manned activity in space. It will make space customary, something in which many people take part and that all Americans share.

Even at its conception SDI is the creation of American society. SDI is a response by one part of the American ethos to national need. Pushing national security into space, while debated as an appropriate means, does indicate the return of traditional objectives of national security. These goals do not, however, demand a "comprehensive" defense, including a massive civil defense effort. They do not require an absolute defense, which is generally conceded to be impossible. The traditional American ethos seeks to enhance security simply by creating a strategic context removed from the inevitable culmination in U.S.-Soviet war: mutual assured destruction.

For it is the linkage of MAD to national security that is unacceptable to most Americans. Even "limited damage" as an objective is unacceptable, for it implies that the most that U.S. strategists can achieve is a slight moderation of wholesale death. Defenses are an alternative. Americans are not so simpleminded that they demand a perfect defense. Rather, they demand only that the defense of U.S. allies and interests is disconnected from their destruction by nuclear weapons. The goal of strategic defenses would be to shift the parameters of a potential U.S.-Soviet war to an arena removed from this country. Mutual assured destruction would no longer be a part of national strategy: it would be a capability without a mission, or a role.

American goals for SDI, then, reflect society's increasing rejection of absolute objectives—whether assured destruction or perfect defenses. The American way of war has been dominated by absolute objectives. In part, assured destruction gained public legitimacy because it flowed from familiar national myths. The most powerful of these came out of the Civil War, America's true total war. Assured destruction has its cultural roots in the dark strategic landscape of Ulysses S. Grant. Grant equated war with revolution. War would be fought for absolute objectives. War would be total, for political stakes could not be compromised. It is an American cultural truth that absolute weapons emerge from, and eventually serve as the instrumentality of, a strategy with absolute objectives. The United States has twice entered absolutist struggles, in 1861 and in 1941.

The world after 1945 was a world of trampled vintage, haunted by the shadows of 1865. American strategists spoke in terms of absolute weapons, of total war, and of political "crusades." Both the Civil War and World War II could demand total national commitment, for war would bring more than peace. It promised moral reconstruction: the reform of society and the world. Nuclear weapons have made impossible a heroic rerun of the traditional American crusade. Yet nuclear weapons remain. As absolute weapons, they are linked in the American mind to absolute objectives even if these are reduced to an official "assured destruction."

They cannot be made into pragmatic weapons, and they cannot be used in reasonable and limited ways.

For three decades most Americans accepted this world of "twilight struggle." Now they seek a safety mechanism, a counter-instrumentality that might separate the symbiosis between absolute weapons and the nuclear fulfillment of absolute objectives. Americans have become more comfortable, in contrast, with the strategic world of Alfred Thayer Mahan, or at least the national cliché of the man. And just what is this world?

- It is a world in which American safety is secured offshore. The battles to protect Americans are fought far from U.S. soil.

- It is a world in which U.S. military forces control U.S. security. They do not simply dissuade an enemy from attacking. They can prevent an enemy from attacking.

- It is a world in which the weapons of war are limited in the damage they can inflict. Although of enormous power, these weapons are specialized. Their power is useful only when directed at other, similar weapons.

- It is a world, therefore, in which the consequences of a war can be contained.

Mahan was the antithesis of Grant. His strategic vision sought security through negotiation for advantage. Potential enemies would bargain for limited national goals through a common medium of exchange. In Mahan's time, this strategic currency was the battleship.[68]

This strategic arena is possible only when adversaries agree. The Mahanian world sought limited war for limited political gains and losses. Such an arrangement was preferred to the alternative: a war with revolutionary goals. It is representative of a world in which adversaries seek advantage at the margins in preference to risking mutual destruction. It may be argued that this process is already under way between the United States and the Soviet Union.

The evolution of such a world, however, has been arrested by the continuing potential utility of absolute weapons. Even in the absence of a workable strategy for nuclear use, the pursuit of nuclear advantage continues to inspire the pursuit of absolute objectives. Americans would like to change this incentive, and strategic defenses could be the lever of change.

CONUSION

It is important to look at the Strategic Defense Initiative and national security through the widest lens. National security is not a problem at the margins of our lives. Nor do the issues of national security exist in "pragmatic" isolation from society. What is— including the esoterica of national security—emerges from what was. We are what our ancestors made us, just as what we will be reflects their vision. The forms of our behavior, including the doctrines we call strategy, are shaped by those who came before.

The Strategic Defense Initiative is such a child. It was born of change in the nuclear world. But the nuclear world was meant to be changed. Thirty years of effort could not blend nuclear use successfully into our national ethos.

A convergence of external pressures, national failure, and acute diplomatic disappointment destroyed a postwar suspension of disbelief. Since 1950 the United States has tried to play the role of a European great power. This has been possible only through a predominance of American moral claim.

This claim has been undermined ultimately by a strategy rooted in nuclear retaliation. Three generations have grown and lived under the shadow of this strategy. Now Americans seek to change it, and change is described through unique and traditional·American values.

Strategic defense offers more and less than a defended world. It is not, and probably will never become, a simple shield. There is no hope that it will end U.S.-Soviet competition. But it offers more in that weapons in space can alter the terms of that competition **in ways that satisfy American cultural imperatives** calling for change in the nuclear world.

As space weapons increase in perceived power, the Soviet space response, already conditioned by decades of competition in space, will tend to mirror U.S. efforts. As space weapons are linked to the achievement of advantage in the overall strategic balance, much of the overt dynamics of superpower competition could be transposed beyond the earth's atmosphere.

Space could come to be seen as the appropriate arena for such competition. In the postwar past the center stage of an actual enactment of that competition would have reached its climax on home territory as nuclear weapons hit silos or cities. The slow evolution toward an eventual exo-atmospheric arena would force abandonment of the need even to threaten nuclear use against cities. The dreaded silos themselves would become irrelevant. The primary goal of shifting strategic emphasis from offense to defense would be the negation of the military **and** the political utility of the ICBM.

Americans are coming to accept what has been called a "conventionalization" of war. If Star Wars helps to promote a perceptual shift from reliance on nuclear security to conventional defense, this would be consonant only with trends already well established in the West. MAD has already become symbolic. But MAD will not become a culturally defused symbol until it is actually, doctrinally, militarily unseated by strategic defenses. This is the importance of SDI. It cannot ameliorate the strategic competition, but it can change the cultural symbolism that is the currency of national will to something Americans can support and embrace.

Add to this trend the Soviet response to SDI. The Soviet Union believes that Americans can make a U.S. SDI a reality. They will dream as long as they can of stopping it forever, but essentially they are resigned to its inevitable evolution. Can they think otherwise in the face of the "scientific-technical revolution" and "the law of dialectic negation"? They have recast their strategic effort to match, if not to counter, the U.S. push for advantage in space.

The Soviets have an ambivalent sense of America. Their belief system decrees that U.S. society is soft. However, unlike the Nazis, who ignored the truths of World War I in their judgment of

America, the Soviets know from experience that the United States is soft only until it decides to mobilize its energies. Soviet myths of America have shaped the Soviets' vision of the future. The United States has made weapons in space **the future**.

It must be restated that strategic defenses will not end the superpower competition. Nothing can do that. But the United States in recent years has faced the daunting prospect of playing the superpower game on Soviet terms. SDI is a very American response.

Today's presentation of strategic defenses is a way of changing the strategic rules of the game. Former responses to Soviet military programs on both the strategic and theater levels seemed insufficient. They neither restored confidence in deterrence nor replaced it with a confident alternative. SDI is a public program that sidesteps a direct nuclear response. It creates in the minds of the Soviets an expectation that their ICBMs may eventually be neutralized. This is a potential—to negate many of the Soviet gains in the strategic balance made in the past decade—but it does not by definition disadvantage the Soviets. They have the means to hold back U.S. strategic superiority, to pursue their own counters in the form of a mix of offensive and defensive systems. SDI cannot turn the Soviet Union into a third-rate power. The Soviets recognize that they have more to gain by continuing to compete, even in space, than by initiating a vain attempt to hold back a historical process they believe to be inevitable. The Soviet Union will stay competitive. The West will merely be competitive once again.

SDI has not yet emerged as a national great debate. In part this stems from the fact that there are no real systems, no hard-cash programs to argue. Indeed, the administration, in the wake of the Reagan vision, has insistently undercut that vision by calling SDI a mere "research program." It has actually laid the groundwork for a more attainable initial goal than the "defended world": that of a reinterpretation of the basis for U.S.-Soviet strategic relations.

However, there were compelling reasons why Reagan called for so much. Reagan was forced, unlike his postwar predecessors, to face a dangerous twin erosion of national will, gnawing away through an unwanted strategy of classical nuclear deterrence and a Soviet push for nuclear advantage that might at last undermine the strategy itself.

In response, Reagan sought a deus ex machina, a divine-like technological hand that would sweep the very need for competition away. That is, perhaps, too much to ask. In place of a defended world, however, strategic defenses can create another form of strategic competition. Americans would prefer it to the assumptions underlying nuclear deterrence. It may be imperfect, but it is perfectly within the galaxy of values defining the American ethos.

So the visible public hub of the issue, the technical feasibility of SDI, obscures the issue. The real problem is not technology. It is public acceptance of change, and a willingness to pursue a course of change. SDI is a lever of historical and strategic change. Technology will follow. It may take twenty or thirty or fifty years.

But the world is already altered. The perpetual norm of a stable nuclear balance of terror is dead. It remains to act upon change to achieve national goals. People look to the future. They hope for a different world. Strategists may prefer to see defenses as mere strategic modulation. People see a release.

There has always been some acceptance of war in the life of society. During the last forty years, however, the prospect of a war has become unacceptable. Worse than unacceptable, cultural drift has come to link nuclear utility with inevitable nuclear use. The mechanism of deterrence seems to have become indissolubly linked to its failure. The basis for nuclear security is now a cultural oxymoron. It is a riddle puzzling to the West, in part because those with the capacity to explain it are themselves often seduced by the moral imperative of its dismantling.

A world restrained to limited war objectives, that has returned to classical power relationships, may seem atavistic. Is the spirit of the age so foolish that it believes it can escape nuclear truth? Can any technology deliver us from the nuclear world? It is a revealing symptom of change, however, that both public and strategic communities again find acceptable the old notions of military power—those that existed before Hiroshima. Perhaps the need for an absolute weapon paralleled the political need—in the wake of a global war against evil—to deter an enemy implying another absolute evil.

What seems clear is an unraveling of the center and its central doctrine. The center may be poised today for a political comeback, but its strategic formulations will differ from those of the postwar pragmatists, the champions of nuclear utility. The pragmatists' search for security through a kind of nuclear universalism was ultimately unfounded. The nuclear doctrines of the pragmatic center were a concatenation of postwar circumstances and world war truths. The pragmatists' "answer" to the questions of national security was their own. It worked for them, and it was successful on its own terms. It did not succeed, however, in passing on its assumptions and its language to a generation of Americans untouched by Pearl Harbor and Munich and Yalta.

If the postwar pragmatists are to reassert their strategic doctrine, they must embrace changes in American worldview. The original presentation of nuclear deterrence was made within the basic framework of the national belief system. The recognitions of global war had made Americans more receptive to an absolutist strategy embodied by deterrence. Pragmatists developed deterrence in a social context still receptive to a kind of national "crusading" mission. That context has changed. A reemergence of more traditional American attitudes, intermingled as they are with an acceptance of postwar commitments, encourages changes in strategic doctrine.

But the basis for that doctrine is unchanged. The United States is as vulnerable today as ever to attack, and no future defense could guarantee Americans from all nuclear threats. Strategic defenses, however, can be shaped to achieve apparently contradictory goals. They can shift the strategic balance, if only glacially, away from nuclear dominance while at the same time actually enhancing the concept of deterrence cemented in the traditions of the nuclear world. Defenses are a way of meeting both the cultural and the military imperatives of national security.

NOTES

1. For a further discussion, see Michael Vlahos, "Cultural Variation, Strategic Planning, and War Performance," American Political Science Association conference paper, August 1985.

2. See Michael Vlahos, *America: Images of Empire* (Washington, D.C.: The Johns Hopkins Foreign Policy Institute, 1982).

3. My use of the term "progressive" is unrelated to the brief, formal era of the Progressive party, and it should be detached from the more persistent, informal usage of the descriptive "progressive" in Left or neo-Left circles before and after World War II.
The religious roots of both purifier and progressive worldviews have been addressed by a number of American scholars. For example, see Perry Miller, *The New England Mind: From Colony to Province* (Cambridge, Mass.: Harvard University Press, 1953); also, Perry Miller, *The Puritans* (New York: Harper & Row, 1963); Sidney Ahlstrom, "The Puritan Ethic and the Spirit of Democracy," in George L. Hunt, ed., *Calvinism and the Political Order* (Philadelphia, Pa.: Westminster Press, 1965).
William Wolf underscored this slow process of religious to secular metamorphosis when he wrote of Abraham Lincoln,

> The Puritan background of Lincoln's confidence in American destiny under God had become rationalized in the nineteenth century into the dream of world democracy with the original religious perspective rapidly disappearing into the distance...[but] Lincoln sustained that vision in its original religious rootage and reference to God's will. ("Abraham Lincoln and Calvinism," in Hunt, *Calvinism and the Political Order*)

This rooting is especially direct in American pacifism.

The major pacifist sects that were transplanted to America had begun as outgrowths of the great religious movements that transformed the intellectual climate of...northern and central Europe in the sixteenth and

seventeenth centuries. Mennonitism and its offshoots formed the radical
wing of the Protestant Reformation, which at the beginning was collec-
tively known as Anabaptism, and the Quaker Society of Friends, for all
the differences that set it apart from the parent movement, was a genuine
child of mid-seventeenth century English Puritanism. (Peter Brock, *Pacifism
in the United States* [Princeton, N.J.: Princeton University Press, 1968], 3)

4. Woodrow Wilson reacted strongly to media criticism during his intervention in Vera Cruz, and his reply resonated to this inner virtue in Americans.

I never went into battle...but I fancy...that it is just as hard to do your
duty when men are sneering at you as when they are shooting at you....
The cheers of the moment are not what a man ought to think about, but
the verdict of his conscience and of the consciences of mankind.

In his very declaration of war in April 1917 he showed that means will remain proportionate to ends as long as unique American moral values rule the
uses of force.

Our object...is to vindicate the principles of peace and justice in the life
of the world against selfish and autocratic power.... We are now about
to accept the gage of battle with this natural foe of liberty.... We are
glad...to fight thus for the ultimate peace of the world and for the libera-
tion of its peoples.... The world must be made safe for democracy.

Quoted in Robert Dallek, *The American Style of Diplomacy* (New York: Alfred A.
Knopf, 1983), 70, 84–85.

5. Roosevelt's powerful vision of America and world order emerge in two
recent, sympathetic interpretations by Burton and Collin. (See David H. Burton,
Theodore Roosevelt: Confident Imperialist [Philadelphia, Pa.: University of Penn-
sylvania Press, 1982] and Richard H. Collin, *Theodore Roosevelt, Culture, Diplomacy,
and Expansion* [Baton Rouge, La.: Louisiana State University Press, 1985]). Beale's
classic is more critical but of course views Roosevelt from the vantage of the
mid-1950s. (See Howard K. Beale, *Theodore Roosevelt and the Rise of America to World
Power* [Baltimore, Md.: The Johns Hopkins University Press, 1957]). At that point
the United States seemed to have learned all the right lessons on the issue from
two world wars, and Roosevelt could be presented as a representative of a failed
paradigm of "imperialism." The newer interpretations see more continuity between Roosevelt and succeeding American approaches to the world. He becomes
at once an authentic spokesman of American values and a visionary of the
American future.

6. *Writings and Speeches of Daniel Webster*, vol. 16 (Boston, Mass.: Little, Brown
& Co., 1903), 423. Also, Frederick Merk, *Manifest Destiny and Mission* (New York:
Vintage Books, 1966); Richard W. Van Alstyne, *The Rising American Empire*
(Chicago, Ill.: Quadrangle Books, 1965); Robert L. Beisner, *Twelve Against Em-
pire: The Anti-Imperialists, 1898-1900* (New York: McGraw Hill, 1968); Ernest May,
Imperial Democracy (New York: Harcourt Brace Jovanovich, 1961).

7. Some of these issues are reawakened in Eliot Cohen's *Citizens and Soldiers:
The Dilemmas of Military Service* (Ithaca, N.Y.: Cornell University Press, 1985). The

true Jeffersonian cast of the purifiers is captured by the words of Thomas Jefferson, who clearly linked republican virtue with "the necessity of obliging every citizen to be a soldier; this was the case with the Greeks and Romans and must be that of every free state." (148) The leveling process of citizen soldiering is underscored in the same book by Ralph Barton Perry.

> That which most entertained and impressed the country was the spectacle of the rich man or the favored of fortune digging trenches with a pick or otherwise deliberately submitting to unaccustomed toil and strange hardships. People read about it because it was funny, but they saw what it meant. They saw that the spirit of service could redeem physical labor from ignominy, and sweep away the external differences and inequalities that divide a man from his fellows.

This was written by one of the founders of the Plattsburg military camps. A professional military, in contrast, would smack of European militarism and monarchism. Instead of leveling, it would discriminate. Instead of promoting republican virtues, it would foster sinister elitism.

8. The observer on this occasion was Joshua P. Blanchard. (Brock, *Pacifism in the United States,* 690.) This can also be said of pacifist-universalist leftists in Germany in August 1914. Such conversions are temporary and fade when the crisis blows itself out. So the conversion of purifiers attained after 1941—as in 1861—has dissipated over cold war time and Vietnam disenchantment. Today, purifier attitudes are resurgent.

9. Manfred Jonas, *Isolationism in America, 1935–1941* (Ithaca, N.Y.: Cornell University Press, 1966). The Ludlow Amendment, introduced by Senator Thomas P. Gore of Oklahoma on August 31, 1917, was the first attempt to introduce a constitutional amendment requiring a national referendum before a declaration of war. Similar proposals were made in every subsequent Congress, except the sixty-sixth.

The Ludlow Amendment and its clones, although sponsored by stolid conservative legislators, were also supported by the Women's International League for Peace and Freedom, the National Council for the Prevention of War, and the Brotherhood of Locomotive Firemen and Engineers, among others.

The spate of House and Senate resolutions in the 1930s attempting to limit U.S. involvement in a war is retro-reminiscent of the "nuclear freeze" era burst of parliamentary high rhetoric. It is worth noting that both periods of rhetorical self exaltation came at times of increasing tension abroad and increasing domestic unwillingness to counter these threats with defense dollars. (Jonas, *Isolationism in America,* 158–64.)

"Ludlowism" has revived recently in the form of this gem of a concept, highlighted by *The New York Times.* Jeremy Stone, director of the Federation of American Scientists, in the Fall 1985 issue of *Foreign Policy,* recommended that presidents be required to obtain the consent of a congressional committee before ordering the first use of nuclear weapons. *The New York Times,* "Nuclear First Use is Revived as Issue," September 9, 1985.

10. A recent brochure of the High Frontier fixates on the vulnerability of the United States to attack.

Picture this...

It is 4:45 a.m. Sunday morning in the
nation's capital...

The streets are nearly deserted.
Washington seems asleep and quiet...

...Except in the Security Room of the
White House and the War Room in the
Pentagon, which are in near chaos.

After twenty minutes of confusion and
conflicting information, they have just
received 100% confirmation by satellite and by radar that six Soviet ICBM's
have been launched from Yedrovo, a
Soviet missile base at the edge of
the Arctic Circle.

They are headed for America.

Etc., etc. But the intriguing aspect of this fearful vision, actually indistinguishable
from the antinuclear motifs of the Left, is its reaching for core myths in the
American experience. How else to explain an early Sunday morning attack, à la
December 7, 1941? Or the arrangement of words, as though they are a kind of
verse in another American tragedy?

11. Richard Falk, "one of the philosophers of the freeze movement," carefully
scolded the moderate purists.

Most current action within the peace movement is dedicated...to *stabiliz-
ing* rather than *eliminating* nuclearism. The goal is to shift from certain
adventurist forms of nuclearism...toward some variant of a *defensive*
nuclear posture.... [But]...reliance on nuclear weapons inevitably con-
centrates anti-democratic authority in governmental institutions and builds
a strong permanent disposition to engage in ultimate war as to negate
the atmosphere and structure of genuine peace. We can never taste real
peace again until we find the means to eliminate nuclear weapons
altogether. (Quoted in Adam Garfinkle, *The Politics of the Nuclear Freeze*
[Philadelphia, Pa.: Foreign Policy Research Institute, 1984], 5)

12. The term, "postwar pragmatists," should not be confused with more nar-
row political designations, like Garfinkle's "pragmatic center" in *The Politics of
the Nuclear Freeze*. The postwar pragmatists embraced most of the foreign-policy
community after 1950, after Taft and Wallace vestiges of another age were
banished. They maintained superficial domestic party attachments, but they shared
a common strategic worldview.

13. Robert E. Osgood, *Ideas and Self-Interest In America's Foreign Relations*
(Chicago, Ill.: The University of Chicago Press, 1953). Osgood describes the
emergence of an American strategic worldview by placing postwar conditions
in a broad context of American historical behavior. He articulates the need for
a pragmatic vision to avoid a return to prewar immobility in U.S. foreign policy.

14. William Broad uses the old metaphor of evil science to show how science enslaves the young engineers engaged in America's dark Star Wars sorcery, entrancing them, as Mephistopheles, to sell their souls for alchemic secrets.

High-tech Gulags such as O-Group (a subdivision of Lawrence Livermore Laboratory) are seductive. They push science and technology to the limit and impose none of the terrible physical privations of their Soviet counterparts. But in some respects they may be more insidious. The prisoners are there of their own accord, serving both science and war, creating in order to destroy, part of any elite, yet pawns in a terrifying game. (William Broad, *Star Warriors: A Penetrating Look into the Lives of the Young Scientists Behind Our Space Age Weaponry* [New York: Simon and Schuster, 1985])

15. Tina Rosenberg, "Mission Out of Control," *The New Republic*, May 14, 1984, 18–21. These sentiments, in slightly milder form, are also echoed in James A. Van Allen, "Space Science, Space Technology, and the Space Station," *Scientific American*, vol. 254, January 1986, 32–39, and Alex Roland, "Triumph or Turkey?" *Discovery*, November 1985.

16. See, especially, "Remarks by Secretary of Defense Robert S. McNamara Before United Press International Editors and Publishers," San Francisco, California, September 18, 1967, printed in *Scope, Magnitude, and Implications of the United States Antiballistic Missile Program*, hearings before the subcommittee on military applications of the Joint Committee on Atomic Energy, 90th Cong., 1st sess. (Washington, D.C.: GPO, 1967), 107.

The more frequent question that arises in this connection is whether or not the United States possesses nuclear superiority over the Soviet Union.

The answer is that we do. . . .

Furthermore, we will maintain a superiority over the Soviet Union for as far ahead in the future as we can realistically plan.

17. These ideas were presented in a September 1967 speech by Robert S. McNamara.

What is essential to understand here is that the Soviet Union and the United States mutually influence one another's strategic plans. Whatever their intentions, actions—or even realistically potential actions—on either side relating to the build-up of nuclear forces necessarily triggers reactions on the other side. It is precisely this action-reaction phenomena that fuels the arms race. . . .

The result has been that we have both built up our force to a point that far exceeds a credible second-strike capability against the forces we each started with. In doing so neither of us has reached a first-strike capability. (Robert S. McNamara, "The Dynamics of Nuclear Strategy," speech of October 9, 1967, Department of State Bulletin, #57)

18. Colin Gray insists that "contemporary arms control theory was an invention of the strategic studies community in the period 1958–60." *Strategic Studies and Public Policy* (Lexington, Ky.: The University of Kentucky Press, 1982), 72.

By the end of McNamara's tenure at the Department of Defense, the theoretical "doctrines" of the public policy community had permeated fully the official strategic worldview. From McNamara's 1967 San Francisco speech:

> We do not want a nuclear arms race with the Soviet Union...what we would much prefer to do is to come to a realistic and reasonably riskless agreement with the Soviet Union, which would effectively prevent such an arms race...since we now possess a deterrent in excess of our individual needs, both of our nations would benefit from a properly safeguarded agreement first to limit, and later to reduce, our strategic nuclear forces. (Printed in *Scope, Magnitude, and Implications of the United States Antiballistic Missile Program,* 109)

19. Stephen Rosen suggests some of the ways in which the existential postulates of strategic theory permeated the conduct of war in Southeast Asia. See Stephen Peter Rosen, "Vietnam and the Theory of Limited War," *International Security,* Fall 1982 (VII/2), 83–114.

20. The words are those of Steve Leeds, of the War Resisters' League, quoted in Garfinkle, *The Politics of the Nuclear Freeze,* 7. These sentiments became legitimate within more "centrist" intellectual circles. Robert Karl Manoff, a sometime editor of *Harper's Magazine,* laid this national corruption at the feet of "nuclearism."

> Thirty-eight years after Hiroshima, it is time to come to grips with the central political fact of modern American life: the epistemological structure of the nuclear regime is incompatible with the epistemological structure of democracy itself. Nuclearism and democracy embody antagonistic ideals of knowledge.... This suggests a disturbing but unmistakable conclusion: The United States cannot long endure as both nuclear and democratic. (Quoted in Garfinkle, *The Politics of the Nuclear Freeze,* 26)

The accession of these attitudes to the highest levels of the old establishment can be measured in the words of George F. Kennan, as he accepted the Albert Einstein Peace Prize in 1981.

> But we must remember that it has been we Americans who, at almost every step of the road, have taken the lead in the development of this sort of weaponry. It was we who first produced and tested such a device; we who were the first to raise its destructiveness to a new level with the hydrogen bomb; we who introduced the multiple warhead; we who have declined every proposal for the renunciation of the principle of "first use"; and we alone, so help us God, who have used the weapon in anger against others, and against tens of thousands of helpless non-combatants at that. (Quoted in Robert F. Drinan, *Beyond the Nuclear Freeze* [New York: The Seabury Press, 1983], 159)

The revisionists themselves are assessed in Robert James Maddox's *The New Left and the Origins of the Cold War* (Princeton, N.J.: Princeton University Press, 1973).

21. This unraveling within the pragmatic center is well covered in Gray, *Strategic Studies and Public Policy,* 129–33, 160–67, and by Lawrence Freedman, *The Evolution of Nuclear Strategy* (New York: St. Martin's Press, 1983), 344–51, 354–58.

22. The fundamentalist tone of contemporary antinuclear films is underscored by the number of video experiences targeted on children and nuclear war: *Bombs Will Make the Rainbow Break, In the Nuclear Shadow, There's a Nuclear War Going on Inside of Me, What Soviet Children Are Saying About Nuclear War.* (From a list in the "Nuclear War Prevention Kit," [Washington, D.C.: Center for Defense Information, 1985]).

It should be remembered also that the nuclear films of the very early nuclear age did not scold or preach. They simply presented the terror of nuclear war as a kind of fact of life. Neville Shute's *On the Beach,* for example, a nuclear movie of the 1950s, was extremely "civilized." Sure, the world was coming to an end as a result of nuclear war. But there was a kind of majesty to the ending of humankind: the very process of attenuation was a dramatic opportunity to unearth the core issues of human existence in the face of extinction. The viewer was left to his own conclusions, and agenda. This sense of fatalism permeated the visions of the 1950s. Rod Serling's "Twilight Zone" episode, "Incident on Maple Street," employed the motif of nuclear war again as a vehicle, a means for exploring the human condition.

23. Jonathan Schell, *The Abolition* (New York: Alfred A. Knopf, 1984), 163.

24. Frank Donner wrote that "opponents of the freeze [are] all paladins of unlimited weaponry...committed to the modern secular religion of a long, twilight struggle with the Soviet Union." This characterization infected some in Congress. Fortney Stark (D.-California) thundered, "[Our people] do not want to be incinerated so some Dr. Strangelove theorist can test his belief that nuclear war is winnable." Tom Harken (D.-Iowa) weighed in with, "No longer will the people of the United States allow their lives to be held in constant peril by the decisions of an elite group of generals, politicians, and scientists." See Garfinkle, *The Politics of the Nuclear Freeze,* 15, 25.

25. "Study Says 4 Billion Could Starve in 'Nuclear Winter' After Attack," *The New York Times,* September 13, 1985. Dr. Mark Harwell, coauthor of the report by the International Council of Scientific Unions, wrote: "We are left with images of Ethiopia and the Sudan as being more representative of what the world would look like after a nuclear war for most of the people than the sorts of images we have of Hiroshima and Nagasaki." The chairman, Sir Frederick Warner, added: "The potential environmental damage of a nuclear war demands that we develop a new perspective when considering such a conflict.... This effort represents the consensus of a prestigious body of scientists. It would be a grave error to ignore their findings."

The more celebrated Nuclear Winter personality, Carl Sagan, makes sure to remind us of the rogue variables that might unleash a nuclear war, variables over which the enlightened have no control.

And in the present time, there is certainly the possibility that some concatenation of communications failure, computer malfunction, misapprehension, madness in high office, could conspire to produce this global climatic catastrophe. ("World Chronicle," taped June 5, 1984, UN Radio and Visual Services, Department of Public Information, transcript, 3-4, 7)

26. National Council of Catholic Bishops, *The Challenge of Peace: God's Promise and Our Response: A Pastoral Letter on War and Peace* (Washington, D.C.: The United

States Catholic Conference, 1983). See also, Episcopal Diocese of Washington, *The Nuclear Dilemma: A Draft Report of the Committee of Inquiry on the Nuclear Issue* (Washington, D.C., August 1985).

Edward Doherty, one of the principal advisers to the bishops, was angered by an article in *Policy Review*. In a letter, published in the Winter 1986 issue, he wrote:

> In refusing to legitimate nuclear deterrence, I argued that I did not will all the horrible consequences that might flow from nuclear disarmament, but did argue that they were nowhere near as horrible nor as permanent as those that would ensue in a major nuclear exchange.... Mr. D'Souza's reporting of this whole conversation exposes his lack of interest in moral discourse and the basic chauvanism of his approach to security questions: The United States is justified in employing any measures, including the use of nuclear weapons, to frustrate Soviet aggression. This may seem to him and to many other Americans as the only practical, realistic policy, but that does not make it square with traditional Christian ethics. (6–7)

Russell Shaw, secretary of public affairs, USCC, added this illuminating perspective for those who wrote for the bishops.

> Someone might object that it is morally obligatory to retain the nuclear deterrent, considering what might happen (loss of political and moral liberties). This, however, is not an ethically coherent argument. We are morally responsible for the evil we will do (or, as with deterrence, that we will to be done on our behalf). But we are not morally responsible for—guilty of—the evil that is done to us, even though we may foresee it as a consequence of our own ceasing to do evil. I am obliged to cease being willing to do evil to an adversary even though I may anticipate that the adversary will then do evil to me. (Ibid., 7)

27. Former secretary of defense Harold Brown put it this way.

> We would not want the Soviets to make the mistaken judgment, based on their understanding of our targeting practices, that they would be spared retaliatory attacks on their territory as long as they did not employ strategic weapons or attack U.S. territory. (Department of Defense, *Report of Secretary of Defense Harold Brown to the Congress on the FY 1981 Budget*, January 29, 1980, 92)

This was couched in "an era of nuclear equivalence." Extension of disproportionate response, many have argued, was a bit more comfortable in an age of assumed U.S. superiority.

28. Much of this was conceded officially. See, for example, the testimony of William J. Perry, undersecretary of defense for research and engineering, in *Department of Defense Authorization for Appropriations for Fiscal Year 1979*, hearings before the Senate Committee on Armed Services, 95th Cong., 2d sess. (Washington, D.C.: GPO, 1978), 980.

29. William T. Lee, "Soviet Nuclear Targeting Strategy" (unpublished paper), 2.

30. Marshal N. Ogarkov, *History Teaches Vigilance* (Moscow: Voyenizdat, 1985).

31. Lieutenant General G. Sememov and Major General V. Prokhorov, "Scientific-Technical Progress and Some Questions on Strategy," *Military Thought*, no. 2, February 1969, found in Lee, "Soviet Nuclear Targeting Strategy," 8–9.

32. As Harold Brown described the "countervailing strategy":

We have concluded that if deterrence is to be fully effective, the United States must be able to respond at a level appropriate to the type and scale of a Soviet attack. Our goal is to make a Soviet victory as improbable (seen through Soviet eyes) as we can make it. (Department of Defense, *Report of Secretary of Defense Harold Brown*, 68)

33. As William J. Perry characterized the limitations of the latest terrestrial BMD system, the LoAD, to defend a "thin" MX deployment in fixed silos:

The last time I made a careful evaluation of it, I believe that it was or could be designed to be capable of extracting a 2-to-1 or perhaps a 3-to-1 cost from the Soviets wanting to attack our silos...I have never seen the evidence which would suggest that we could with confidence extract any higher cost...therefore, the question about a LoAD system, in my judgment, is not whether it works or does not work. The question is...will it do you any good defending 36 silos or 50 silos or 100 silos? In my judgment, the answer to that is no. (*Strategic Force Modernization Programs*, hearings before the subcommittee on strategic and theater nuclear forces, Senate Committee on Armed Services, 97th Cong., 1st sess. [Washington, D.C.: GPO, 1981], 483)

34. *Diplomatic and Strategic Impact of Multiple Warhead Missiles*, hearings before the subcommittee on national security and scientific developments, House Committee on Foreign Affairs, 91st Cong., 1st sess. (Washington, D.C.: GPO, 1969); *Strategic and Foreign Policy Implications of ABM Systems*, hearings before the subcommittee on international organization and disarmament affairs, Senate Committee on Foreign Relations, 91st Cong., 1st sess. (Washington, D.C.: GPO, 1969), especially statements by Drs. George B. Kistiakowsky, Hans A. Bethe, Herbert York, and James R. Killian.

35. On implied potential of BMD in 1981, see *Strategic Force Modernization Program*, hearings before the Senate Committee on Armed Services (Washington, D.C.: GPO, 1981).

36. On the more esoteric issue of data processing, see the testimony of the SDIO panel on computing in support of battle management, summarized in "Panel Affirms Feasibility of Producing SDI Software."

The software for a battle management system capable of meeting the requirements of the Strategic Defense Initiative is well within the reach of current technology, computer specialists who have studied the problem told the Senate Armed Services' subcommittee on strategic and theater nuclear forces. (*Aviation Week & Space Technology*, December 9, 1985)

37. George Keyworth thinks that an aerospace plane, or SCRAMJET (Supersonic Combustion Ramjet), could eventually be able to lift orbital packages 1/100 of the payload cost of the space shuttle: from $2,000 to $20 per pound. Even a factor of ten reduction would be necessary, however, before the erection and logistical support of a space weapon's architecture would be "cost-effective." George Keyworth, "American Interests," Program #514, The Blackwell Corporation, Neal B. Freeman, executive producer, 1985.

38. Harold Brown, "SDI Technology and SDI Policy," 19, speech before IISS conference at Windsor Park, October 15, 1985.

39. Ronald Reagan, television address, March 23, 1983.

40. Paul Stares, *The Militarization of Space: U.S. Policy, 1945–1984* (Ithaca, N.Y.: Cornell University Press, 1985), 225.

41. From FDR's "Quarantine" speech made on October 5, 1937, in Chicago, an isolationist bastion:

If those things come to pass in other parts of the world, let no one imagine that America will escape, that it may expect mercy, that this Western hemisphere will not be attacked and that it will continue tranquilly and peacefully to carry on the ethics and the arts of civilization. . . .

If those days are not to come to pass—if we are to have a **world in which we can breathe freely and live in amity without fear**—peace-loving nations must make a concerted effort to uphold laws and principles on which alone peace can rest secure. (Emphasis added)

42. Some of the interplay between postwar presidents and domestic pressures over issues of war and peace is discussed by Charles DeBenedetti, *The Peace Reform in American History* (Bloomington, Ind.: Indiana University Press, 1980).

43. Charles Mohr, " 'Star Wars' in Strategy: The Russian Response," *The New York Times,* December 17, 1985.

44. Ibid.

45. Tom Krebs and Associates, "Soviet Costs to Counter GDABM Using Destructive Countermeasures and Additional Warheads," April 15, 1986. The study includes additional Soviet warheads and destructive countermeasures. "Early Threat DCM Systems (IOC 1991–1993)" include space mines, space fragment clouds, direct ascent ASAT, space kinetic-energy weapons, and ground-based lasers. The "Later Threat DCM Systems (IOC 1995–2000)" include space high-energy lasers, fast-burn nuclear weapons, pop-up X-ray weapons, space X-ray weapons, air-based lasers, and space NPB (Neutral Particle Beam). The scope of a Soviet countermeasures effort would be so great that "costs to the Soviets to counter GDABM would be prohibitive, even to achieve the most minimum of objectives."

46. Michael Vlahos, "A Crack in the Shield: The Capital Ship Concept Under Attack," *The Journal of Strategic Studies,* (II,1), May 1979, 47–82.

47. Joel Setzen, "The French Doctrine of the Offensive" (Ph.D. diss., University of Chicago, 1981).

48. Mohr, " 'Star Wars' in Strategy."

49. Steven L. Rearden, *History of the Office of the Secretary of Defense: The Formative Years, 1947-1950* (Washington, D.C.: GPO, 1984).

50. The incident and its intelligence aftermath is nicely related in Fred Kaplan, *The Wizards of Armageddon* (New York: Simon and Schuster, 1983), 156–60.
Colin Gray admits the public impact of the incident on some government figures but qualifies its influence.

> The bomber gap, to my knowledge, made no notable impression upon the civilian strategic studies community. Civilian strategists seem to have been profoundly unimpressed by the concern of some Democratic senators and Air Force generals in 1955-56 over the projected deployment rates for the Tu-95 Bear and the Mya-4 Bison. The Study of Airpower Hearings of 1956, carefully stage-managed in an election year by Senator Symington, evoked no debate among the new civilian strategic theorists. (Gray, *Strategic Studies and Public Policy*, 65)

But the political climate was highly inflected by the awkward Soviet strategic bombardment force, and its voice predominated.

51. This point was underscored by U.S. reaction to the first, primitive Soviet systems. See Gray, *Strategic Studies and Public Policy*, especially Gray's discussion of Rand reports R-266 and R-290 on 42, 65.

52. Some of this evocative imagery is self-conscious among purifiers.

> It has long been hoped that humanity, humbled by the immensity of space and comparative minuteness of the earth, would finally abandon its military and imperial ambitions. . . . To those members of the first living generation to view the earth from space, their planet seemed small, fragile, and solitary, an oasis in a void otherwise profoundly hostile to life. The image of 'the Whole Earth' became an icon...the image resurrected in a new form the ancient Earth Mother goddess. . . . 'The cult of space' today has its roots deep in the strategy of world domination through global terror pursued by the Nazis in World War II. (Jack Manno, *Arming the Heavens: The Hidden Military Agenda for Space, 1945-1995* [New York: Dodd, Mead, 1984], 1, 2, 5)

The mélange of Christian and pagan symbolism—icon, earth mother goddess, resurrect, cult—is blended, however, into a kind of Manichaean, coeternal struggle between good and evil. Like many American purifiers, their sense of lineality is uninformed.
The Manichaean struggle between good and evil is intrinsic to purifier worldview. In a book just published by Harper & Row (ergo, legitimate), *Star Wars and the State of Our Souls*, by Patricia M. Mische, there are chapter titles like "Vader vs. Skywalker: The Movie's Real Message," and "Fascination with Technology

and the Faustian Bargain." For a constituency whose conscious sense is highly secular, their common language of strategic discourse strives for the sacred.

53. Stares, *The Militarization of Space*, 18.

54. Author query of Harold Brown, January 1986.

55. *Anti-Satellite Weapons, Countermeasures, and Arms Control*, summary, Office of Technology Assessment (Washington, D.C.: GPO, September 1985), 10. As the Reagan administration maintains:

> Orbiting overhead are over 800 Soviet satellites, compared to some 400 satellites of the West. That is a ratio of 2 to 1, and unlike in the West, the vast majority of Soviet satellites are military. (From an address by Robert C. McFarlane before the Overseas Writers Association, Washington, D.C., March 7, 1985. Printed by the Bureau of Public Affairs, United States Department of State, Current Policy no. 670)

56. Stares, *The Militarization of Space*, 71.

57. Ibid., 72.

58. Lieutenant-General Ferene Szues, speech to a national conference, entitled "Capitalism in the 1980's: Crisis and Search for Solutions," *Nushadscrel*, February 23, 1985, 9; quoted in Daniel Gouré, "Soviet Strategic Planning and U.S. Strategic Defense Initiative" (a paper delivered at the 53d Symposium of the Military Operations Research Society, June 1985), 38.

59. Ogarkov, *History Teaches Vigilance*.

60. Minister of defense and marshal of the Soviet Union, A.A. Grechko, speech, *Krasnaya Zvezda*, March 21, 1973, 3; quoted in Gouré, "Soviet Strategic Planning."

61. Marshal of the Soviet Union and minister of defense, Sergey Sokolov, answers to questions of TASS correspondent, *Krasnaya Zvezda*, May 5, 1985; quoted in Gouré, "Soviet Strategic Planning," 44.

62. Gouré, "Soviet Strategic Planning," 22–23.

63. The latest Soviet developments are briefed in U.S. Department of Defense, *Soviet Military Power*, 5th ed. (Washington, D.C.: GPO, 1986), 41–48.

64. A. Krasikov, "For a Peaceful Cosmos," *Izvestiya*, June 16, 1982, 2; quoted in Gouré, "Soviet Strategic Planning," 45.

65. Gouré, "Soviet Strategic Planning," 5.

66. Charles H. Fairbanks, Jr., "Arms Races: The Metaphor and the Facts," *The National Interest*, Fall 1985, 75–90.

67. Stares, *The Militarization of Space*, 72.

68. In this context I am referring to Mahan's broad impact on native visions of national strategy. Mahan's slogan on the influence of sea power changed the way in which Americans thought about national security. Most Americans were not aware of Mahan's more "European" ideas about the life and interests of nations. Mahan was interpreted in the embrace of American uniqueness, and his transatlantic brand of historicism remained eclectic.

For works by Mahan, see, especially, *The Influence of Sea Power Upon History, 1660–1783* (Boston, Mass.: Little, Brown & Co., 1890); *Lessons of the War with Spain* (Boston, Mass.: Little, Brown & Co., 1899); *Naval Administration and Warfare* (Boston, Mass.: Little, Brown & Co., 1908); *The Interest of America in International Conditions* (Boston, Mass.: Little, Brown & Co., 1910); and *Naval Strategy Compared and Contrasted with the Principles and Practice of Military Operations on Land* (Boston, Mass.: Little, Brown & Co., 1911).

Other Publications of
The Johns Hopkins University
Foreign Policy Institute

FPI POLICY STUDY GROUPS

Trade Policy: Three Issues, Isaiah Frank, ed. (1986), $5.00
U.S.-Soviet Relations, Simon Serfaty, ed. (1985), $5.00

FPI POLICY BRIEFS

Arms Control: A Skeptical Appraisal and a Modest Proposal, Robert E.
  Osgood, April 1986, $3.95
Thinking About SDI, Stephen J. Hadley, March 1986, $3.95
The French Fifth Republic: Steadfast and Changing, Simon Serfaty,
  February 1986, $3.95
Mexico in Crisis: The Parameters of Accommodation, Bruce Michael Bagley,
  January 1986, $3.95
The Middle East: Timing and Process, I. William Zartman, January 1986,
  $3.95
Summit Diplomacy in East-West Relations, Charles H. Fairbanks, Jr., Oc-
  tober 1985, $3.95
*The Gandhi Visit: Expectations and Realities of the U.S.-Indian Relation-
  ship*, Thomas Perry Thornton, May 1985 (out of print)
Lebanon: Whose Failure? Barry Rubin, May 1985 (out of print)
Living with the Summits: From Rambouillet to Bonn, Simon Serfaty and
  Michael M. Harrison, April 1985 (out of print)

SAIS OCCASIONAL PAPERS

America: Images of Empire, Michael Vlahos (1982), $4.75
Tilting at Windmills: Reagan in Central America, Piero Gleijeses, Carib-
  bean Basin Studies Program (1982) (out of print)
American and European Approaches to East-West Relations, Robert E.
  Osgood (1982), $3.95
A Socialist France and Western Security, Michael M. Harrison and Simon
  Serfaty (1981), $4.75

SAIS REVIEW

Biannual journal of international affairs, $7.00 (subscription prices vary)

To order copies of these publications contact the FPI Publications Program, School
of Advanced International Studies, The Johns Hopkins University, 1740
Massachusetts Avenue, NW, Washington, DC 20036 (202-332-1977)/*SAIS Review*
(202-332-1975).

WESTVIEW PRESS/FOREIGN POLICY INSTITUTE

SAIS PAPERS IN INTERNATIONAL AFFAIRS

1. *A Japanese Journalist Looks at U.S.-Japan Relations*, Yukio Matsuyama (1984), $14.00
2. *Report on Cuba: Findings of the Study Group on United States–Cuban Relations*, Central American and Caribbean Program, ed. (1984), $8.50
3. *Peacekeeping on Arab-Israeli Fronts: Lessons from the Sinai and Lebanon*, Nathan A. Pelcovits (1984), $24.00
4. *The Evolution of American Strategic Doctrine: Paul H. Nitze and the Soviet Challenge*, Steven L. Rearden (1984), $19.50
5. *Nuclear Arms Control Choices*, Harold Brown and Lynn E. Davis (1984), $10.50
6. *International Mediation in Theory and Practice*, Saadia Touval and I. William Zartman (1985), $31.00
7. *Report on Guatemala: Findings of the Study Group on United States–Guatemalan Relations*, Central American and Caribbean Program, ed. (1985), $12.00
8. *Contadora and the Central American Peace Process: Selected Documents*, Bruce Michael Bagley, Roberto Alvarez, and Katherine J. Hagedorn, eds. (1985), $32.00
9. *The Making of Foreign Policy in China: Structure and Process*, A. Doak Barnett (1985), $22.00 (hardcover)/$10.95 (softcover)
10. *The Challenge to U.S. Policy in the Third World: Global Responsibilities and Regional Devolution*, Thomas Perry Thornton (1986), $30.00
11. *Defending the Fringe: NATO, the Mediterranean, and the Persian Gulf*, Jed C. Snyder (forthcoming)
12. *Fiscal and Economic Implications of Strategic Defenses*, Barry M. Blechman and Victor A. Utgoff (1986), $22.75
13. *Strategic Defense and the American Ethos: Can the Nuclear World Be Changed?* Michael Vlahos (1986)

To order copies contact Westview Press, Customer Service Department, 5500 Central Avenue, Boulder, CO 80301 (303-444-3541). All prices are subject to change and do not include postage. VISA and Master Card accepted.

SAIS REVIEW

VOLUME 6, NUMBER 2
SUMMER–FALL 1986

MONEY, DEBT, AND DEMOCRACY

Reforming the Exchange Rate System
C. FRED BERGSTEN

Monetary Policy and the Debt Crisis
ENZO GRILLI

Bold Canadian Initiative: Free Trade
TIMOTHY J. NAFTALI and PETER O'HAGAN

Ruminations on the Reagan Doctrine
GEORGE LISKA

Europe's Own Theater Missile Defense
HUGH DE SANTIS

Disaccord on Southern Africa
DAVID F. GORDON

Qaddafi's Calculated Risks
MARY-JANE DEEB

MORE THAN A JOURNAL, A RESOURCE!